D0864962

HAUNTED CHIPPEWA VALLEY

DEVON BELL

HAUNTED
America

Published by Haunted America

A Division of The History Press

Charleston, SC 29403

www.historypress.net

First published 2013

Manufactured in the United States

ISBN 978.1.60949.977.8

Library of Congress CIP data applied for.

I dedicate this book to the love of my life and best friend, Tony.

CONTENTS

PREFACE

Surely there had been no figure leaning on the back of his chair; no face looking over it. It is certain that no gliding footstep touched the floor, as he lifted up his head, with a start, and spoke. And yet there was no mirror in the room on whose surface his own form could have cast its shadow for a moment; and, Something had passed darkly and gone!
—Charles Dickens, The Haunted Man

Ever have that feeling that you aren't alone? It starts with an odd noise that makes you whip your head around with nervousness. Maybe you think you just felt a light wind on the back of your neck making the goose bumps pucker and stand up. Or perhaps a flash of something dark was captured out of the corner of your eye. You know that there is no one there and you are safe. But are we ever really, truly alone?

There are many possibilities as to why locations all over the world could be haunted: spirits of men who died a violent death on the battlefield and whose souls are forever attached to the spot where they died; an individual who passes away in his home and does not want to leave in death; a victim who was viciously murdered and is trying to communicate with anyone living so she can help avenge her death. Along with actual ghosts or spirits, I have always thought that some places simply have energy in certain areas, whether it is good or bad.

Along with energy, history is around us all everywhere we go. Here in the Chippewa Valley, we have a rustic old history of lumber barons, Native Americans, fur traders, explorers canoeing up and down the many different rivers and trains rumbling along the old rusted tracks. German and Norwegian settlers came here in search of a better future for their families. They tended the lands with careful hands and planted the seeds of what we can now today see in our local historical museums. What one can't see in these museums are the secrets and horrific stories that have also planted a seed of many ghosts who inhabit different areas throughout the Chippewa Valley.

In 2011, I was perusing the Internet and slightly bored, so I thought I would pay a visit to the Unexplained Research discussion forum. Once I had logged in, I clicked on the category that said, "Wisconsin Ghosts." I started scrolling through the different topics, and one caught my eye and made me stop dead in my tracks. It was a thread called, "Bloomer Massacre." I immediately started reading about this. I grew up and spent a great deal of my life in Bloomer, Wisconsin. Nothing ever happened in Bloomer; I always thought it was the most unexciting place ever. I have learned throughout my experiences in legend tripping, paranormal investigating and writing about these locations that you should never judge a book by its cover and that any peaceful place can definitely have a dark past.

With history comes mystery, and like I always say, "Without history, there would be no ghost lore." I'd like to invite you to come with me now, and let's explore the histories and mysteries of the Haunted Chippewa Valley.

ACKNOWLEDGEMENTS

I would like to start out by saying thank you to my wonderful husband of nearly five years, Tony. You are my best friend and greatest supporter, and you always encourage me to delve into anything I have an interest in. Thanks to my parents, Lance and Peggy, who have always told me I can do anything I set my mind to. My friends and family are all great supporters, and without their encouragement and, oftentimes, input, I probably never would have started writing!

Thank you to Ben Gibson at The History Press for giving me this wonderful opportunity. Thanks to Terry Fisk for all your knowledge and help and for telling me about this great series, Haunted America, and also for pointing me in the right direction. For Chad Lewis, I owe a great deal of thanks for answering every little e-mail I have ever sent his way and helping or guiding me in the best possible way.

I would also like to thank Robin Melland from the University of Wisconsin Stout Archives; you have always been there ready and willing to help, and I admire how much passion and drive you have for history. Also thanks to the University of Wisconsin–Eau Claire Archives, the L.E. Phillips Memorial Library in Eau Claire and also to the La Crosse Public Library. During the process of writing this book, I had many contacts that helped me in my research, whether it was historical or paranormal. First, thanks to friend/paranormal investigator/author Chris Wiener for more information on the sordid history of Chippewa Falls. To Brad Sundell, who I hold in such high regard when it comes to history, thank you for all of your help when researching the Evangelical Cemetery. I truly admire all the hard work you put into this cemetery, which will not be forgotten by many, I can assure you. I can't forget to leave out psychic and friend Tamara for sharing openly her personal stories and also thanks to Sharon from the Cornell Library for sending me some great photos and historical information regarding the library.

I very much appreciate all the individuals from whom I received historical photographs. Thanks to Chris Schlais for sending me photos of Mary Schlais. To Gene at the Irvine Ghost Pub, thanks for your stories and help. Last but not least, a very big thank you to the Eau Claire City Hall for the use of so many historical photos that really captured the essence of Eau Claire many years ago.

I also want to say thank you to all those individuals who took the time to share either historical information or their own personal stories on any of these locations via the Internet that were referenced in this book. Many people helped me in my quest during this process, and I apologize if I have neglected to thank someone of the utmost importance to me. If this is you, please accept my deepest apology and know that I am so very grateful for all the help that went into the creation of this book.

CHAPTER 1

SPIRITS OF THE CHIPPEWA VALLEY

I don't know how many times I have heard the joke referring to every town or city in the state of Wisconsin consisting of churches and bars all lined up next to each other in a neat row. Many of these places—be it church or bar—have been a part of a town's history for quite some time. Residents still occupy the old wooden pews in the local church. The "townies" still hang out at the local tavern or pub, gossiping about anything and everything. But late at night when the doors are locked, the lights are down and no living soul is around, that's when shadows play on the walls and the spirits of the dead come out to play.

THE SHEELEY HOUSE

Chippewa Falls, Wisconsin, has somewhat of a violent past connected with the logging boom, including many fires that burnt down several buildings, boardinghouses and dozens of railroads as well. There is one building that was lucky enough to escape the wrathful flames that claimed many stores and shops. Situated on the corner of West River Street and Pine Street is the James Sheeley House. The building is a wonderful example of the Victorian elegance of the late 1800s. According to the official website for the Sheeley House, "At the height of the logging era, it was one of thirty boarding houses that furnished a home to loggers, railroaders, drifters, and adventurers." Before the Civil War, the first buildings were erected where the Sheeley House sits today. In 1868, a man by the name of Carl Hering purchased the property and moved his family into a small house on River Street. Mr. Hering's carriage and blacksmith shop were located behind his house. In 1884, a man named John B. Paul, who operated a boardinghouse about a block away, purchased Hering's property from him. Paul tore down the carriage and blacksmith shop, surfacing the entire building with red brick. The Paul House had a saloon on the ground floor, living quarters on the first floor and a nice-sized kitchen along with the boarders' dining room and second-floor bedrooms. A gentleman by the name of James Sheeley, an Irish immigrant, stayed at the Paul House while he was working on the railroad from Wabasha, Minnesota, to Chippewa Falls. Sheeley was a lumberman who was in failing health and could no longer work such a strenuous job, so he and his family decided to settle down into a more peaceful lifestyle. In 1905, he and his wife, Kate, bought the Paul House. James tended the bar while Kate and their children, Anna, William and Howard, cooked and cleaned rooms. Even after James passed away in 1913, his wife still served meals and rented rooms out but leased the bar. After Kate's death in 1934, daughter Anna no longer served meals but still rented rooms to boarders. By the year 1981, Anna finally had to leave her home of seventy-six years. At that time, David and Sharon Raihle decided to restore the last boardinghouse still standing in Chippewa Falls. This couple did in-depth research, comparing old photos and mapping out every single detail of how the building would have looked in its prime. A fellow named Jim Bloms had heard of the James Sheeley House when it was shut down, and in 2001, he decided to purchase it, having had many years experience in the hospitality and tourism field.

The history of the James Sheeley House seems like many other historic locations all over the country. Many people who have purchased old buildings choose to restore them to their former glory. The Sheeley House really does shine, and when driving past it, you can't help but stop and stare, admiring it for its Victorian charm. However, there is a dark side to this location, one that is oftentimes not spoken aloud among the locals. A good friend of mine, Chris Wiener, is a paranormal investigator and author. He wrote a book called *Haunted Chippewa Falls* and really shed new light onto the reported paranormal activity at the James Sheeley House. Every summer he gives a grisly tour of Chippewa Falls, and the Sheeley has been the main focal point where the tour starts and ends. Wiener has some disturbing tales regarding this location, and it seems to me that there just might be some restless spirits who are tied to this place.

According to Wiener, he states that during the time the Sheeley was a boardinghouse, "lumbermen came to meet 'all' of their needs. They ate, slept, drank and fornicated in the halls of the establishment." River Street back in its heyday was lined with boardinghouses and hotels, and many of them could be described as houses of ill-repute. When it was called the Hering House, there was a window that was red with a single candle placed in the center of the glass. When the candle was lit, that meant a lady was ready for her next "customer." Another interesting tidbit is that during the time James Sheeley and his family owned the establishment, it was a speak-easy during Prohibition. There are articles that can be found in the *Chippewa Herald* reporting on law enforcement busting the saloon for serving alcohol, even to minors.

That's just the beginning. Kate Sheeley passed away in 1934 due to a horrible accident. There is a set of narrow wooden steps on which she tripped and fell down. Due to her injuries, she never recovered and eventually died. Years later, many have reported seeing her apparition standing at the top of those very same steps, located on the second-floor dining room. These deadly steps have been roped off to protect others from the same fate Kate met. After daughter Anna's passing in a local retirement home back in 1992, some have claimed to have seen her spirit walking aimlessly along the halls. Perhaps she just could never let go of her beloved home. Anna's ghost has been seen by many, but some have seen her as a child, some as an adult and some even as an elderly woman. Current owner James Bloms explained that since he took over the business, there has been supernatural activity from the very beginning. He and other employees have heard phantom footsteps, encountered floating silverware and dishes and have also heard disembodied voices. One worker claimed he was locked in a freezer and after about a half an hour was able to pick the lock and get out.

Historical buildings such as the James Sheeley House are a testament to how long a place can withstand the test of time. History lovers such as the Raihle family had the passion to restore the old boardinghouse to its former glory after it had sat vacant for many years. It's very admirable to put heart and soul into a project like that. Unfortunately, sometimes when we unlock the old rusty door, spirits may rise from their eternal slumber. In the case of the Sheeley House, it seems as though the energy or spirits that remain simply feel content to peacefully reside with the living. But make no mistake; they will do what they can to prove they are still there.

IRVINE GHOST PUB

A few miles from the James Sheeley House heading west on County Highway X, then turning onto Fleet Street, there is another "spirited" bar called the Irvine Ghost Pub. If you can't tell, the current owner embraces the lore along with his business and invites paranormal teams and curious bystanders to step into the creepy, claustrophobic basement where ghostly activity is reported to take place. Just like the Sheeley House, this place was also used for a boardinghouse. Unlike the Sheeley, though, this particular tavern is wrought with a very violent crime from the past: a heinous murder the spirits there haven't let go of and want to remind every person who walks through the front door why they are still there.

Friend and author Chris Wiener gave me the inside scoop on this location as well. He and his paranormal investigative team, the Chippewa Valley Paranormal Investigators, were all very familiar with this joint. They investigated it numerous times and had some interesting tales to tell. At the time Chris and his group first started checking things out, it was called Eisold's Irvine Bar and was under different management. The business itself is located next to railroad tracks and started out as the Beanery Hotel in the 1860s and then turned into a general store in the late 1800s. Railroad workers would come to this place to purchase supplies and also to eat at the lunch counter that was a part of the store. Eventually, the upper level of the building turned into a boardinghouse for young men who were traveling through. The men would sit and have a "cold one" while awaiting their next venture for the ever-booming lumber business. The lunch counter eventually became a bar and the general store a saloon. According to Chris Wiener's book *Haunted Chippewa Falls*, "The Irvine Hotel in its many forms and owners saw several turnovers, such as the McDonalds owning the hotel in 1910 and making a try of it as a restaurant. This led to it becoming Irvine Bar and Grill."

With a tumultuous past in Chippewa Falls, it's not shocking there are ghost lore legends sprung from real-life crimes. Case in point is the murder of Allen Holm. In 1965, Mr. Holm bought the business and turned it into the Irvine Bar. Allen, or Al, as he was better known, ran the bar for many years up until the evening of January 15, 1986. In the early morning hour of around 4:00 a.m., seventy-one-year-old Al was viciously attacked and murdered in his apartment, which was situated above the bar. According to Wiener, "The police reports say it was one of the grizzliest murders in Chippewa." Poor Al was stabbed numerous times in the head, neck and chest, and some reported that his blood covered even the ceiling of his apartment. According to a

The Irvine Bar, circa 1940s. *Photo courtesy of Gene Beecroft.*

1986 news article, Holm had suffered from diabetes and had other health issues. His lower legs were amputated about fifteen years prior. The man convicted of Al's murder was twenty-three-year-old Michael Potts. Potts reportedly told police officials that killing Al was a "big kind of killing thrill." According to police lieutenant John Liddell, the young Potts stated that "he hoped the death would provide peace and tranquility for the family." As a result, public defender Dennis Sullivan entered pleas on Michael Pott's behalf of not guilty and not guilty by reason of mental disease or defect. Chris Wiener told me personally that Potts is currently serving a twenty-five-year to life prison sentence for the murder but will be up for parole very soon. Did Potts really commit this crime as a mercy killing? Or were there other dark disturbing reasons? This we may never know. During his life, many say that Al was a jokester and loved to play pranks on friends and family. Many say that in death, nothing has changed.

Patrons of the bar have reported the feeling of someone tapping on their shoulder, but when they turn around, no one is there. The prankster spirit also has tugged on peoples' hair, vying for their attention to let them know he is still around. Like many bar owners, Al had his own special spot where he liked to sit: a red bar stool located where the counter curves close to the men's restroom. Many who have sat in this particular stool have seen the spirit of the murdered bartender looking at them, but when the individual prepares to vacate the stool, Al simply disappears. At the end of the night when the current bartender puts all the stools up on the tables to clean, they come back to find Al's stool sitting back on the floor, rooted in its proper place.

In 2008, a couple bought the bar and called it Eisold's Irvine Bar. They started renovating and claim that strange things started happening almost immediately. When they were in the basement of the bar with their young son, he started waving at some unseen presence and went on to tell his parents that he saw another young child down there. This had happened on numerous occasions after the son's first encounter with the spirit child. The Chippewa Valley Paranormal Investigators have encountered shadows of a male figure, orbs, strange voices on audio recordings and also Al himself. On one investigation, Chris and his team decided to communicate with Al. They knew he had been a smoker in life, so they sat at the bar and lit up a cigarette, placing it in an ashtray. They then asked him to take a couple puffs for them and to their astonishment, they saw the tip of the cigarette turn a cherry glow four or five times, almost as if someone were taking drags off the cigarette. Chris speculated this could have been caused by certain air movement inside the bar, making the cigarette light up repeatedly.

There is also the existence of a young ghost child named Ellie. While conducting EVPs (electronic voice phenomenon) on a different investigation, they caught a voice that said, "Elsie would have died at birth." After that, they started to address the spirit as Elsie, not Ellie.

According to Wiener, there was supposedly a young girl, between the ages of four and six years old who had passed away many years ago, and he speculates this young ghost girl could be the little girl who passed on. Whether she died at the bar or near the location is still undetermined.

The current owner is Gene Beecroft, who decided to embrace the paranormal activity and name it the Irvine Ghost Pub. Perhaps that is what the ghosts wanted all along—just to be heard and for the living around them to be at peace with their presence there. That's good, because I don't think these rambunctious spirits will be going anywhere anytime soon!

STONES THROW

Venturing over to the city of Eau Claire and heading to the downtown area, there sits an old majestic building that stands strong and proud. I admire this solid stone structure with its beautiful Romanesque appeal and Gothic design. I admire it because, after all these years, it refuses to budge. Looking up at the turret and then at the grey stone façade, it almost looks like something out of a medieval film. Many photographers flock to it, snapping away, and I sometimes think it winks back at them, loving the added attention. The Stones Throw is remarkable in its charm and elegance. But don't judge a book by its cover.

When this building was first erected in the years 1893–94, it was called the Cameron-Drummond-Slagsvold Building. The most prominent commercial tenant to first inhabit the building was a bank. According to the book *Sawdust City* by Lois Barland, "The Chippewa Valley Bank was organized in 1876 by Henry C. Putnam. It was reorganized in 1885. It stood on the corner of Eau Claire and Barstow and in 1904 had a capital of $100,000 and a surplus of $10,000." In the year 1906, the bank consolidated with the Bank of Eau Claire and the Mortgage Loan and Security Company. The main part of the bank was located on the corner of Barstow and Grand, and the branch office was located on the corner of Eau Claire and Barstow. Another large commercial company that resided in this building was the Samuelson Department Store, but after 1906, it was known as Union Savings Bank. It is now called the Stones Throw and has been a pub for years serving patrons beer, wine and perhaps "spirits" of its own.

Authors Chad Lewis and Terry Fisk covered the Stones Throw in their book *The Wisconsin Road Guide to Haunted Locations* and explained the legend of a man who supposedly took his life by hanging himself in the building in the early 1900s. Ever since it became a bar/restaurant, there have been stories of strange happenings in the basement. To date, investigators Lewis and Fisk were unable to verify the suicide. Some employees talk of whispered voices or footsteps heard when they are alone in the bar. Beer bottles will violently shatter of their own accord, and objects seem to be misplaced, which irritates the staff there. One chilling tale came from a bartender several years ago. He said that he was getting ready to close up for the night and jokingly said out loud, "Okay, everybody out!" At that precise moment, a figure who, up until that time had gone unnoticed, stood up from his chair, shook out his jacket and walked to the front door, where he vanished right before the shocked bartender's eyes. Immediately after that, the employee left and never returned to his job.

A resident explained that this bar was owned by her relatives a few years ago and had a terrifying tale to tell. This person said she always felt like there was something "off" about the bar, almost that there was more to that place than what meets the eye. She also stated that in the early twentieth century, it was a jazz and blues club. Having heard the story of the man who hanged himself, she then asked a relative about this. The relative went on to tell a slightly different story about a man who was murdered, saying his body was then dragged downstairs to the basement. After the bar was closed up, lights would come on by themselves and the owners figured it was the spirit of the murdered

Chippewa Valley Bank, circa late 1800s. This building is now the Stones Throw. *Photo courtesy of the Eau Claire Landmarks Commission.*

man. People have even reported seeing the ghost's reflection when peering into a mirror that is situated behind the bar.

It seems as though there are many accounts of unusual activity at the Stones Throw. Behind the beautiful trim and design of the building lurk many mysteries and secrets. Was there a man who was murdered and then dragged to the basement? If so, perhaps that is why employees have felt cold chills and foreboding feelings while down there. I implore my readers that if ever they are in the Eau Claire area and feel like stopping in for a drink, head on over to the Stones Throw. Take in the beautiful old building, and enjoy a beer while relaxing on one of the bar stools. Just make sure the person sitting next to you isn't a restless spirit!

HOUSE OF ROCK

Our last stop is the Water Street district in Eau Claire. This area is filled with students from the University of Wisconsin–Eau Claire and also families with their children and pets strolling along the slabs of sidewalk and playing over in the nearby park. If you aren't familiar with Eau Claire and the college area, you may find yourself driving around aimlessly and perhaps turning onto Water Street. You could easily miss this particular bar, nestled between other businesses. But if you look closely, 422 Water Street is the cradle of this establishment, with an interesting look to the exterior of the building. After visiting for the first time, I chuckled because I could see the rock exterior on the front and thought, now that's fitting for its name! Most often during the day, the old tavern sits dark and dormant. But perhaps this is just an illusion, as there have definitely been ghostly accounts from past patrons and employees. Oh yes, there's a darker side to this place called the House of Roc—a darkness that creeps in on you when you least expect it.

For the most part, the history of this bar is pretty vague. The only history I could dredge up was two former names: the Oar House and the Light House. According to the bar's website, "It was important to keep the word 'house' in the name to keep alive part of its history. Now, it's the House of Rock featuring top bands playing some of the hottest rock and blues this side of the Mississippi." One of the House's famous drinks is its Bloody Marys. Mix that with some great music, and you've got a fun-filled night for sure! So it seems there is a theme with this bar, with the word "house" always having been a part of the name. Maybe this is because this place "houses" spirits of its own. If you look past all the energy, stage lights, music and people, there's a sinister past to be found.

According to an online article from the Unexplained Research website, many of the bar employees have a lot of respect for the infamous ghost of the bar, Al Morgan. Al was a former owner back in the early 1980s when it was called the Oar House Tavern. The story goes that one night Al kicked a regular patron out of the bar because of some gambling issues, and later, this person came back to the bar with a shotgun, cornering Al at the bottom of the basement steps, shooting and killing him on the spot. A slightly different version of events was that a jealous boyfriend or husband shot another man to death at the bar. With this story in hand and the help of Robin Melland from the University of Wisconsin Stout Archives, I started some digging of my own and was able to find the name of the person who killed Al, as well as some other details from that dramatic day.

It was a day just like any other day until a strange man entered the Oar House Tavern. The date was Wednesday, April 15, 1981, and it was around 12:30 in the afternoon when Gerald Jacobson sat down and started to drink. Fifty-one-year-old Albert Morgan, the owner of the Oar House Tavern came in around 1:30 p.m. that very same afternoon. Al stopped to chat with bartender Greg Cramer and then headed toward the basement, where his office was located. He was planning on putting several new pool table covers out and needed to go down to his office to get them. At this point, another employee, Doug Indahl, saw this strange man from the bar get up out of his seat and start to follow Al to the basement. Indahl thought it odd because

Al had one strict rule, which was that no one who was *not* employed at his bar was allowed down into the basement. The employee was perplexed and started to walk over to the basement door when he heard a noise that he described as a firecracker. When he opened the door, Gerald Jacobson was there and quickly brushed past him and ran out the front door of the bar. When Indahl turned to look back at the basement, he saw Al Morgan lying lifeless at the bottom of the steps. He then made a mad dash for the door Jacobson had just rushed through and attempted to run after him. He called out to the bartender that Morgan had been shot. The bartender hurriedly called the police. Indahl managed to get the license plate number of Jacobson's car to give to the police. Just minutes later, Detective Sturgal spotted the gunman's car heading up State Street and took off after him. The chase finally ended at Jacobson's home on May Street. When Jacobson pulled into his driveway, he left the car running and proceeded to head straight to his father, Francis, who was taking the garbage out. With his .38-caliber revolver in hand, he walked up to his father and fired, ignoring the cries from Sturgal, who could not shoot Jacobson because his father was in the line of fire. According to a news article from the *Eau Claire Leader Telegram*, "The officer reported Jacobson shot his father, turned and took one step towards him, whipped the gun to his head and shot himself." First aid was given to the father, who was taken to Sacred Heart Hospital and survived with only a scalp wound above his right eye. Jacobson died at 2:00 p.m. at the same hospital from the single gunshot wound to his head. Meanwhile, Al Morgan had been transported to Luther Hospital where he succumbed to his injuries. The bullet had gone through his right eye and had penetrated his brain.

After I read the news article, I thought to myself that this almost seemed like a made-for-TV movie. The whole ordeal was very dramatic. People were left wondering why Gerald Jacobson killed Al Morgan and his own father. Thirty-two-year-old Jacobson was an army veteran of the Vietnam conflict, and I wonder if he suffered from post-traumatic stress disorder, like so many other soldiers from Vietnam. He was described as

The basement steps at the House of Rock where poor Al was found shot to death. *Photo courtesy of the Bells' personal collection (a big thanks to Dez for allowing us to take photos inside the bar).*

a "loner" and "messed up," so obviously he had exhibited odd behavior before the shootings. The Eau Claire chief of police reported that Mr. Jacobson had a prior arrest record, including disorderly conduct in 1977. After he shot himself, police found a list in his pocket that had the names of Morgan, Jacobson's parents, his boss at the local gas station and eight other people. Was it possible that he intended on a mass murder that day in 1981? Whatever the details or motives, Jacobson took it to the grave with him. Another question is whether Al's spirit is still within the House of Rock. Perhaps since his untimely demise, he still watches over the bar, wanting people to know he is still there. I received an e-mail back in 2011 from an employee at the House of Rock. He sought me out to tell his story. According to the employee's e-mail:

The stories of Al's murder in the bar and the possibility that he is haunting the bar have always been a popular topic of discussion at the end of the night. We have noticed that in the past couple months, we have been experiencing more unexplained phenomenon than before. Experiences include: hearing voices coming out of the bar's stage speakers when nothing is connected to them, and hearing voices and footsteps from the first floor when standing in the basement when absolutely nobody else is in the bar.

The final spot where Al stood, unsuspecting, before his murder is a hot spot for activity. People have felt a presence near them when no one else is there, so perhaps Al's ghost is still anchored to this area and really wants to communicate with employees so they know he's there. The e-mail from the employee at the bar went on to say:

The current bar manager was in the basement during the day when nobody else was in the bar, and the doors were locked and he heard voices and footsteps on the main floor. When he ran up to double check if he had locked the doors, there was no one in the bar and the doors were indeed locked. I think he said that happened sometime in the past six months.

The same individual told me of an old cooler down in the basement. Twice when walking into it, he got an extremely weird feeling or a sense of energy passing through him.

Essentially, just about every employee, past or present, could tell a story of an odd encounter or chilling experience. The House of Rock will live on, perhaps not only with the living, but the dead as well.

So the next time you go out looking to tip back a few or catch a good local concert, head on down to the House of Rock. You might take in more than just a live show, but a very "spirited" one as well.

CHAPTER 2

CREEPY CARYVILLE

B ack in 2006, a friend and I decided to attend a symphony at the State Theater in Eau Claire, Wisconsin. At the last minute before I left home, I grabbed *The Wisconsin Road Guide to Haunted Locations*, by Chad Lewis and Terry Fisk. I had paged through the book and was intrigued by this little town called Caryville. What was interesting to me was that there were five locations in the general area that are reported to be haunted, and this little town was just outside of Eau Claire. I don't claim to be great when it comes to directions; I'm more of a landmark kind of girl. However, once we got out there, I seemed to drive forever, almost looping in circles, when searching for the old cemetery on the hill. I kept seeing the sign for 240th Avenue over and over again. For a person who ventures out there for the first time, the roads don't really match up, and I started feeling hopelessly lost. Then I came to a fork in the road and decided to go the opposite direction. My friend and I were cruising down a rough country road when I had this feeling or inkling we should turn onto this dirt road. I turned, and we followed it as it curved to the left. Once we got around the curve, there was a dirt driveway. I parked, and we both looked to the left. There it was, the Sand Hill Cemetery.

It was a cold February day, so we glanced about but decided to remain in the warm car. From there, I pulled out of the driveway and took my car down a long, rutted dirt road. We then came upon what looked like a boat landing. I parked, and my friend got out the book to see if we were in the right place. As I was looking around, my friend let out a bloodcurdling scream. Once my heart started pumping again after the scare, I turned to her and asked what made her scream. She replied, "I just saw a big black translucent shadow standing at the back of the car." She then paged through the book until she came to the part about the boat landing. To our shock, we read the story about the black, shadowy demon nicknamed "Blackie" that haunts the area we were in! I drove away, and as we sat in silence, we came upon the old church and schoolhouse. I didn't even bother stopping; I just headed as fast as I could back to Eau Claire. I thought to myself, "Well, welcome to Caryville!"

A few years later, I took my husband out there, and he was as intrigued as I had been. We then decided to produce a full-length documentary on this location. When I did some historical research on the area itself, I found it at times difficult to find certain information and answers. It's sort of ironic, but in my opinion the ghost lore is easier to find than the history, to some extent. I often like to say that perhaps the spirits outnumber the residents here.

Caryville is located in the northwestern part of Wisconsin in the Rock Creek Township, within Dunn County. The small town is unincorporated and was settled in 1855 by Norwegian immigrants. George and Mahala or Martha Pierce moved in 1857 to Fairplay, which was a small ferry crossing site located in the township of Peru, Dunn County. George was very vocal in naming the township he lived in and served as clerk and supervisor. Then in 1866, the Pierces moved to the township of Rock Creek and bought a farm. It wasn't until 1883 that this land was officially named. Mr. Pierce requested a survey be made of a proposed village site that was on his land. The land was then recorded as the "Village of Pierce." A year before the plat for this village was created, there was a post office that had been built and was given the name of Caryville after John W. Cary, who organized the Milwaukee Road Rail line and served on its council until his death. In May 1892, John Cary, who was at this point the president of the Milwaukee Land Company, ordered a new plat, eventually calling the town Caryville, and its name has not since changed. The area was very attractive for its fertile soil, which came from the river bottoms and the creek that drained three miles to the south. Many of the Norwegian settlers who inhabited the town claimed their land and wanted a promising future for their families. By 1888, the town consisted of a feed mill, general store, hotel, post office, school, church, blacksmith shop and Pony Express office, and a train station was situated there by the year 1895. It was very hopeful Caryville would become a larger city, perhaps the size of Eau Claire, but that was not to be. Due to the geological location of the area, including the important factor of not having a ferryboat until 1909, Caryville never fully flourished.

Today it seems little has changed with the small town of Caryville. Driving along Highway 85 over the Chippewa River, this settlement is there and gone in the blink of an eye. Today, this small town consists of a local store, a parking lot for bicyclists who use the Chippewa River State Trail and a handful of homes. There are remnants of what used to be. There is the abandoned line of the Milwaukee Railroad, now utilized as a bike trail, and a few homes that look as though they have withstood the test of time. So why exactly is this small town with only a minute population reported to be haunted? I like to say that perhaps this small town harbors something much more than farmland. Maybe, just maybe, the dead really *do* outnumber the residents here. If Caryville wasn't close to the old town of Meridean located on the Chippewa Bottoms, I often wonder if there would be ghost lore attached to it. You see, Caryville has nothing reported to be haunted within the town itself. There are, however, haunted locations just outside of the town: the Fosbroke School; the Spring Brook Norwegian Evangelical Lutheran Church; the "Phantom Cars of Caryville Road," which is basically a small bridge; the old Meridean boat landing; and the Sand

Hill Cemetery. This sometimes makes it confusing for history buffs or legend trippers when visiting. One would think if people say the town itself is haunted, it would make perfect sense that the hauntings would be within that particular town. This is not the case with Caryville. So without further ado, I want to be your tour guide for the night and take you on a journey to creepy Caryville…

THE FOSBROKE SCHOOLHOUSE

Outside of Caryville sits a tiny white schoolhouse that has been empty for some time now. This one-room school is quaint with its basic small white wooden frame and sits directly across the street from the Spring Brook Lutheran Church. The earliest records of the school are from 1914. It officially shut its doors the summer of 1961 and has sat dormant ever since. Lore tells us of a young boy who used to attend the Fosbroke School many years ago. One version of the story is that on a cold winter day, the boy froze to death in his desk at the school. Another version states the child was running away from his abusive father and ran to the one place he felt safe, the little schoolhouse. Sadly, while hiding inside the school, the young boy froze to death, and the next morning, his teacher found his small frozen body still sitting at his desk. There is another macabre story that weaves the tale of a preacher who killed all the schoolchildren and then took his own life by hanging himself above in the belfry. Some have reported seeing the preacher hanging, his lifeless body swaying back and forth from the deadly noose. A rather disturbing tale is of a girl who was raped by a ghost, and later there was blood splattered all over the walls of the building. There are two ghostly specters that seem to watch over this place. One is a shadowy black demon nicknamed "Blackie." It lurks about the schoolhouse, and if you park your car too close, the dark being will shake your vehicle. A "familiar" in the form of a

The Fosbroke Schoolhouse in 2011 right after some work was done to the building due to all the vandalism through the years. There was a new front door put in along with new shutters that were also painted, and finally a new front porch was constructed. *Photo courtesy of the Bells' personal collection.*

three-legged, one-eyed black cat guards the school and will stare at you with its evil eye if you come too close. The best part of the lore, in my opinion, is the legend that if you go inside the building and sit in the desk of the little boy, you will feel a rush of his spirit or energy pass through you.

In reality, the tragic events that spawned the supernatural tale of the little boy were substantiated by authors Lewis and Fisk. After researching further, they learned there was indeed a young boy named David Grohn who attended the school in the 1950s and did pass away, but not from an abusive father driving him to the schoolhouse one cold winter Wisconsin night. I had the delight of speaking with a former student of the Fosbroke School. She told me she attended school with young David and that he stepped on a rusty nail, which caused a wound that got horribly infected. He ended up with lockjaw from the infection and eventually died from it. He could have either died at home or in a local hospital. Even after learning of the true story regarding the little boy, I still wonder if the old school is truly haunted for perhaps other reasons.

THE SPRINGBROOK LUTHERAN CHURCH

Directly across the street from the Fosbroke School is the Spring Brook Norwegian Evangelical Lutheran Church. In 1871, the Reverend Amund Johnson organized the church congregation, which was located on Happy Island or Old Meridean. Some of the members lived on the north side of the river, and the rest resided on the south side. Reverend Johnson served the congregation until 1872, when Reverend Gzermund Hoyme took charge and served until 1876. In 1875, the first church at Old Meridean was built. Unfortunately, in 1886, the church burnt to the ground, and then in 1889, a larger church was built in its place. In March 1917, the decision was made to split the congregation in two so the members living on the north side of the river would have their own congregation. They started the Spring Brook Lutheran Church, and in 1919, the people of Spring Brook built the church two miles northwest of Caryville, located on the north side of the river, and that is the church that still stands today.

So many tragedies occurred with the congregations, including flooding on Old Meridean where the church stood, and then years later, the church was razed by fire. Could these tragedies have left negative energy and perhaps made it easier for evil to slink in? There are several stories regarding this small country church, one including that of a priest named Jacob. This priest put all his time and effort

The Springbrook Lutheran Church, 2009. *Photo courtesy of the Bells' personal collection.*

into the construction of the building. Reportedly about forty years ago, some investors came into Caryville, wanting to demolish both the church and school. Jacob was so distraught and enraged he took his own life by removing the stairs from inside and hanged himself in the belfry. Soon after, some townspeople spotted his lifeless body hanging in the bell tower. There have been reports since this suicide from either locals or legend trippers who have seen the poor priest's body swinging back and forth in the tower. I think it's a bit odd that both the church *and* school have lore talking about suicides in the belfry. I wonder if one tale was told that led to the other building across the street being saddled with similar lore. Or perhaps one of the locations really had a suicide, but over the years, word of mouth confused the facts and reported the other place instead. That's the trouble with urban legends or ghost lore; you never quite know when or where it came from. I would also like to point out that according to Lewis and Fisk, they stated the "priest" Jacob would not have been a priest since this is a Lutheran church. Locals have also refuted the story of any suicide in or around the church. The authors stated that the ghost lore has actually been around since approximately 1994, not thirty years ago, as it has been reported in other sources.

THE PHANTOM CARS OF CARYVILLE ROAD

A couple miles from the church and school, there is a very small bridge. This is probably the one location without any answers. During my research, I was not able to find any information that could shed light on the ghost lore. On one of my many visits, my husband, Tony, and I actually parked the car at the bridge to get out and take a look around. Tony climbed down the side embankment, taking the digital camera in hand. He found a plaque on the side of the bridge, which read, "State of Wisconsin Department of Transportation." There was also the year

1996, so we can only assume perhaps it was rebuilt that year. Tony also found a plank sticking up and was speculating this was a part of the old or original bridge until it was replaced, but again, I can't state this to be factual. As for the original year it was constructed, I honestly cannot say.

This simple country bridge has a female entity attached to it. According to the legend, a young prom queen named Jenny was driving home from the dance. After a wild night of drinking and partying, the doomed prom queen had become intoxicated, lost control of her vehicle and crashed into the bridge, her car plummeting into the dark water below. Ever since this tragedy, people have reported when driving over, their vehicles will break down or have some sort of mechanical problem. Jenny's car (or red truck, in other versions) has been seen driving up and down the road, and then it vanishes before the bystander's eyes. Due to the phantom vehicle, the bridge has been dubbed "The Phantom Cars of Caryville Road." People cruising along this stretch at night have said that either a car or what looks like a red truck will play chicken with them, trying to run them off the road. Many think this is the ghost of Jenny, seeking revenge after her tragic death. Finally, the most ghoulish tale is at night, if you stop, get out of your vehicle and peer over the side of the bridge, you just might see the faint headlights of the dead prom queen's vehicle shining up through the churning water. I don't know what it is about water and things below the surface, but this story has always given me goose bumps.

Locals vehemently deny anyone ever having been in a fatal crash on or around the bridge. According to paranormal investigator Chad Lewis, though, this is one of the most heavily reported paranormal events people relay to him. These bright headlights will come out of thin air, chase their victim down and then vanish without a trace. I personally feel it could be the headlights of a vigilante because a couple of times I was out there, I've been followed from the bridge to the boat landing, either being tailgated or just followed and almost watched from a distance. Whether this person or persons are local or just feel they need to keep watch remains to be seen.

THE BOAT LANDING

The next location has rich but confusing history at points. There is the boat landing that I mentioned earlier, located down a long, winding dirt road that leads to the Chippewa River or what is also called the "Bottoms." I have seen this place in the spring, summer, fall and winter. I've seen it calm and stormy. I have seen the river low and the sand dunes popping above the surface where fishermen walk out to cast out their lines. I have seen the river flooded, the entire boat landing washed away and the trees almost buried beneath its depths. This place is peaceful yet turbulent. You just have to look beneath the surface to better understand.

There's history that speaks of Native American battles and war, of confusion and paranoia of the white people, and also the explorer Jonathan Carver who set up camp in the area. Like I said, the area is rich in history but shrouded in mystery. In 1858, the pioneers had been raising crops, which were the fruit of their labors and the core of a better future for their families. They settled on what was called Happy Island, which they later named Meridean. A church was built, and the tiny village was mainly a logging community because the town was situated on the river. There were many floods and fires, which killed several individuals, and also accidental drownings as well. On September 30, 1871, the boiler in the shingle mill on the island exploded, which resulted in the death of a sixteen-year-old girl named Nora Nebow, along with her uncle, Peter Aas. Eventually, with the constant flooding, the island town could no longer endure, and Meridean was eventually moved to another location that still exists today. Nature has now taken over the island, and there are little remnants of the town. When I visited it, I could still make out the dirt roads that are now overgrown with weeds.

Mary Dean: her memory is the core of the island's supernatural mystery because, according to local legend, the town was named after her when she passed away. Even though the spelling and pronunciation

Sketch of the old mill located on Happy Island. *Sketch courtesy of John Russell.*

of the town has changed slightly, the main story has not. The story of young Mary Dean is very fascinating, and even though locals and others have stated that she truly existed, there is still no written or recorded proof she was indeed real. There are several versions regarding her story. According to the book *The History of Dunn County*, Mary was quite real. There were a number of tales spun about her and how the place formerly known as Happy Island became Meridean. The first is the more beloved tale, which locals and historians speak of about a little girl who was traveling on a steamboat along the Chippewa River with her mother. The child was loved by all on board. Little Mary and her mother were on their way to be with Mary's father, who already was employed on Happy Island. Tragically, during the voyage, the little girl became ill, and shortly before arriving at their destination, she succumbed to her illness. In commemoration of her, the townspeople gave her a service, and a small coffin was improvised from an empty box. She was then interred beneath a tree on the island, and everyone decided to name their town Meridean in memory of her In 1884, the grave and tree were washed away by a flood.

Unfortunately, there is no proof such as the tree, a grave or marker that proves she really existed. Mary Dean is almost that of an urban legend, and like most urban legends, the tales told of her began to change. In other versions, a young woman named Mary Dean was on her way by ferryboat to the island to meet her husband, whom some have stated was Ira Dean, a gentleman who started the shingle mill there in 1863. She became ill and died before she arrived to reunite with her husband. A slightly different story speaks of a trapper by the name of Dean and his wife, Mary. They both lived and worked on the island, but one tragic day Mary drowned in the nearby slough. After her untimely death, the trappers and adventurers living on the island decided to call the place "Mary Dean." A much darker tale I have come across speaks of Mary as an unsavory character. She had traveled down the river on a lumber raft from a sawmill with a violent group of craftsmen. Later that night, the men got into a bloody brawl, and Mary was viciously murdered. They buried her on the island and named it after her in almost a macabre jest.

As I was conducting new research for this book regarding Mary Dean, I stumbled upon a news article I had never seen before. It was a story that I have never read or heard about, and believe me, I have seen many! This particular article was from the *Eau Claire Weekly Leader* dated Saturday, November 2, 1895. The article states:

> *You folks in Eau Claire do not know how Meridean came to be named as it is. If it was correctly named to the letter, it would be Mary Dean, and the story is, a beautiful maiden was traveling in company with a Presbyterian minister and wife, Mr. and Mrs. Hunter. They were all missionaries and came here in the year "one" to benefit the savages. Mary fell sick coming up on a keal boat [sic], and she died where the old mill stood, 1889 or 1840. The Hunters returned to Quincy, IL.*

Because of this elusive young woman, tales of terror have surfaced from the watery depths of the river. Several people have claimed to have seen a spirit woman who they say is almost like a siren in the water. She will entice you and then pull you under to your watery grave. Many have reportedly seen a glowing woman in white either hovering over the water or walking along the boat landing. I wonder if she is looking for a loved one or awaiting one of the ghost ferries to pick her up. There have been tales of these ghost ferries seen traveling up and down the river. Perhaps the old ferries are still picking up and dropping off the spirits or souls of the inhabitants who at one time lived on the island. Author Terry Fisk told me during his interview for our documentary on the area that water can have its own energy. Many spirits gain this energy from the water itself so they are stronger, and at times, the body of water is seen as a bridge or portal for them to cross over to the other side. Is it possible that this body of water wasn't just used for ferryboat transportation? Is the river a bridge for the dead?

There is another odd story attached to this location. I'd like to take you back to October 24, 1953. A fifteen-year-old girl by the name of Evelyn Hartley was babysitting in her hometown of LaCrosse, Wisconsin, and disappeared without a trace. All these years, her friends and family have continued to look for her. There was even a book written about her disappearance: *Where's Evelyn*, by Susan Hessel. Many rumors floated around, one even being that the infamous murderer Ed Gein had abducted and killed her. Fellow historian John Russell first told me of this case and proclaimed that he didn't think the girl or her remains had ever been found. There was a rumor that Hartley was indeed dead and was buried somewhere in the Caryville/ Rock Falls area. Reportedly to date, this is still a cold case. Ironically, I came across a different story about someone who stated they saw the face of a young woman in the river water or general vicinity near the boat landing. Perhaps the face is that of the spirit of Evelyn Hartley... or Mary Dean.

A more chilling tale is the legend of a young couple who ventured down to the boat landing one afternoon for a romantic interlude. The next day a fisherman found their truck, but the couple was nowhere to be seen. There was blood and some inhuman hairs found inside the truck. Some speculate they met the fate of a hellhound. This supernatural dog can be found in mythology and folklore. The hound oftentimes appears transparent with black fur and glowing red eyes. They move with super speed, possess great strength and are often described as having extra-long, sharp claws. Some say these hounds guard the entrances to the world of the dead and are a great omen for death. Legend also states if a person comes into contact with a hellhound, they are not to speak of it for one year and one day; otherwise the person will die. Another version warns if any individual sees a hellhound three times, they will immediately die. The most dreaded rumor states that after seeing a hellhound, it will come after you and drag you to hell.

The hellhound story came about because of a report of a sanitarium that supposedly existed on Happy Island at one point in time. The doctor who ran the hospital had several dogs. One day the doctor left the island and his dogs behind. Sadly, the dogs were neglected and starved to death. Some say after death, they crossed over to become hellhounds and now roam freely at the boat landing and cemetery atop the hill. A side story tells of the dogs attacking and killing their owner's child as well. The dark demon "Blackie," which hangs out at the schoolhouse, has been spotted at this location as well. There are reports of teen suicides and others drowning in the river, but nothing was ever substantiated. The main dare if you decide to visit is to park at the boat landing at night. Turn off your headlights and wait. A hellhound will supposedly then appear with hellish red eyes and white snarling teeth. But maybe *this* story is too hard to swallow.

THE SAND HILL CEMETERY

The fifth and final stop on our grisly tour is the Sand Hill Cemetery, which is situated atop a hill from the boat landing. At first, there was little information, but after about a month of research I was able to find names and information of the persons buried there. I really connected with this place and admit that now when I see the vandalism, I almost take it personally. The Sand Hill Cemetery is basically a family and neighborhood plot. Either the people buried there are related or lived close to one another. The location is majestic and serene, the perfect place for a soul to rest for eternity. The old decrepit slabs mark the ending of someone's life and possibly mark their afterlife as well.

According to Unexplained Research, locals spoke of two young women who were out at one of the five haunted locations back in the 1980s, most likely the cemetery. One of the women started speaking in tongues and became almost possessed while there. This is when investigator Chad Lewis believes the lore actually started. Reportedly, some have seen strange balls of light hovering above a few of the headstones, and others have heard their own name being whispered

The Sand Hill Cemetery, 2011. *Photo courtesy of the Bells' personal collection.*

by some unseen entity. There are also tales of ghost children who are seen running around the cemetery and nearby field at night. On certain occasions these little spirits are reported to walk right up to people, perhaps trying to be friendly. This cemetery was rumored to have been mentioned on the popular television show *Unsolved Mysteries*, where they were able to document paranormal activity there. This has since been discounted, as there is no proof whatsoever of the Sand Hill Cemetery being featured on the show. Numerous individuals have said they heard growling sounds from the fields and trees, leading them to think the hellhounds are lurking about. Even "Blackie" himself has been spotted here as well. There are the more cliché stories of Ouija boards going off the charts when using them at the old graveyard and that more activity happens on Halloween. There's another tale that can most likely be discounted of another neglected cemetery back in the woods. If you curse or spit on one of the graves, a boxer or other angry dog (perhaps a hellhound) will appear. No one has ever found this other graveyard, and the owner of the land stated there is no such cemetery in existence.

I hope readers enjoyed this rollercoaster ride around Caryville. Whether Caryville, Wisconsin, is simply a normal small town in the Midwest remains to be seen. Locals would tell you that the lore is not true, that it was made up by thrill seekers and used as initiations for their friends. Others might have a darker, disturbing tale to tell. Whether you are a history buff, thrill seeker or both, I personally invite you back to this place anytime you have the desire to visit the strange and unusual. A word of caution if you decide to visit: don't go alone.

CHAPTER 3

BRIDGE OVER TROUBLED WATERS

I remember having a conversation with author/paranormal investigator and friend Terry Fisk in which he told me that water is sometimes seen as a portal for the dead and is a way for them to pass from one side to another. Water also has its own kind of life and energy, which spirits may feed off of and gain strength from. Because many bridges are situated over water, perhaps the spirits or ghosts are somehow connected to these sturdy structures.

Soo Line Bridge

It's always very fascinating to see how many old bridges or structures we preserve and how long they have withstood the test of time. In the late 1800s, the rail line was still the main method of transporting everything from goods to people. Several of these bridges can still be walked upon today and admired for their sound structures. There is a particular bridge in Eau Claire, Wisconsin, that holds not only history but also an appealing view. The Soo Line or "S" Bridge is located right across the street from the Old Uniroyal Tire Factory, now called the Banbury Place. I thought it ironic that this bridge and the old factory are reported to be haunted, perhaps by the same spirit or spirits.

The Soo Line Bridge is called the "S" Bridge because it forms the letter S in shape. The bridge is 442 feet in length, and it crosses the scenic Eau Claire River. In 1910, decisions were made to reconstruct the bridge. Workers used steel beams instead of wooden ones so the structure would be more durable and last longer. A local resident was walking across the bridge a few years ago and stopped to take a picture. Later, when reviewing the photograph, she saw a little ball of light or what people call "orbs." She then did a little digging and found out that a man fell to his death while rebuilding the bridge. The blog that I read by this resident was pretty vague so I decided to go over to the Chippewa Falls Public Library and do some digging of my own. I ended up finding a couple different newspaper articles from the year 1910 that talked about the accidental death.

John Murphy (1862–1910) was a bridge carpenter who lived on East Cedar Street in Chippewa Falls, Wisconsin. He was described as a "sober, diligent man who enjoyed the acquaintance of a large circle of friends." On May 3, 1910, at around 3:00 p.m., forty-eight-year-old Murphy was working on the north end of the bridge, seated on the railing with a handful of his co-workers who, at the time, had their backs to him. It was reported he lost his grip and fell approximately twenty-five feet to his death. His fellow workers were not given much warning as they heard him call out, which followed by a sickening thud down below. Murphy struck his head between two timbers, and after an autopsy, a gentleman by the name of Dr. Lyman ruled the cause of his death as a result of internal injuries. He left behind his wife, Katherine, and daughters: Mary, who was a teacher for the Island Street School (which no longer exists), and Anna, who at the time was a student. This was such a tragic ending to a life so many years ago. After reading about the local resident's ball of light in her photograph, I started wondering if it was possible that John Murphy

The Soo Line Bridge, 2010. *Photo courtesy of the Bells' personal collection.*

has never left the scene of his death. Maybe he has unfinished business to attend to.

The Soo Line is now utilized as a bike and walking bridge and has gorgeous scenery from every angle. I've often thought how sad it is that something so tragic happened there, but perhaps the late Mr. Murphy is able to look down on it and admire what he worked on during his lifetime. The City of Eau Claire decided to restore the bridge again years later to make it even safer for bicyclists and pedestrians. The bridge was presented with the Historical Restoration Preservation Project of the Year Award by the American Public Works Association. This meant that repairs went underway for the "S" Bridge, including ties being replaced, installing a new deck and railing and new concrete added to the piers.

Thinking of John Murphy, maybe he is trying to communicate with certain individuals because he wished to somehow be involved in past repairs, a job he was never able to finish during his life. If his spirit does linger at the bridge, it seems he is a peaceful ghost. I wonder if maybe all he wants is to watch over the place he lost his life for. To add some irony to this story, Murphy is buried with his wife, Katherine, and daughter Mary in the Hope Cemetery located in Chippewa Falls. There are rumors that this very cemetery is also haunted. Could the activity be from the Murphy family?

Take a stroll over this unique bridge and stop to take in views of the city and river below. You just may feel a floral-scented breeze caress your cheek or think you hear the sound of a disembodied voice. Or perhaps you'll catch the flash of something in the corner of your eye. Whatever reason people visit this historic bridge, I know one thing for certain: it will always keep you fascinated.

GREEN EYES BRIDGE

As a child, I used to travel with my parents to visit my cousin Kevin quite frequently. I remember his house, the yard and the way he would catch and tickle me until I was breathless from giggling. Unfortunately, he passed away when I was still a young child, so over the years many memories have faded. Fast-forward to the year 2009; I was out with my husband looking for this haunted spot called the Green Eyes Bridge. When we finally found it, I thought nothing of it, just that it was very peaceful with its location out in the country. There was a point when I mentioned this place to my father, who in turn told me that Kevin lived right across the street from this very bridge.

The Green Eyes Bridge, also known as the "Bridge Over Troubled Waters" or the "Troubled Waters Bridge" is located on Chaney Road in the Town of Bridgecreek near Augusta, Wisconsin. On one of the occasions that my husband and I were there, we happened upon a local resident who informed us that the structure was an old car bridge and that he remembered driving over it with his parents when he was young. Was there a fatal accident or worse that had befallen this old rustic bridge?

Some sources state that years ago during the Great Depression, a black man hanged himself off the Green Eyes. There is also a slightly different tale of a black man who was hanged from the tree by the bridge, but it was a hate crime committed by several white men, possibly from the Ku Klux Klan. Ever since the suicide or murder, he haunts this place. Another horrific tale involves a local Augusta family. One night, the father slaughtered his entire family and then went to the bridge, where he proceeded to hang himself. His ghost has haunted the bridge for nearly one hundred years. Since this shocking crime, people have reported seeing a dark silhouette hanging from one of the girders of the bridge, and it has been thought to be the ghost of one of the supposed suicide victims. In other accounts, many have seen the shape of a body hanging off the side of the bridge, and at night, some have even seen glowing green eyes and exclaim that it's the eyes of the man who murdered his family—hence the name Green Eyes Bridge. According to *The Wisconsin Road Guide to Haunted Locations*, it relays a tale from either 1994 or 1995 when a woman and some of her friends were staying in a cabin near the bridge. After they returned from buying supplies in the nearby town of Augusta, they walked inside the cabin to find ropes tied into nooses and then saw a mysterious shadow draped across the piano. They left in a hurry and never went back to retrieve their supplies or belongings. Along with these sordid stories, I also found information pertaining to the alleged green eyes. After showing pictures to an entomologist named Paula K. Kleintjes, PhD, at the University of Wisconsin–Eau Claire, she determined the glowing eyes were that of firefly larvae or "glow worms." This sheds new scientific light on the green dots or what people thought were eyes on the bridge at night.

Today the Green Eyes Bridge is used mostly by four-wheelers, fishermen and lovers of nature. Any paranormal investigator or legend tripper should check this spot out. Visit during the day, but then come back at night and wait. Maybe you'll see a dark shadow and glowing green eyes of the man who hanged himself on the bridge or just a bare noose blowing lazily in the wind. I came across information on the Augusta, Wisconsin official website that stated, "The Bridge Over Troubled Waters and area had its name long before the Simon and Garfunkel song. At one time, there was a one room schoolhouse named the Troubled Waters School just 3 miles from the bridge." But where exactly did the name "Troubled Waters" come from? Is there some tragic event that took place on or around the bridge that is connected to the waters below? This, along with the ghost lore, may be a mystery forever.

THE OLD TRAIN BRIDGE

A couple years ago, paranormal investigator/author and friend Chris Wiener mentioned a story in his book, *Haunted Chippewa Falls*, that caught my attention. It was with regard to an old train bridge that I'd never given a second thought or glance to when heading out of town. However, after reading what the author had to say, now I always give the train bridge my full, undivided attention.

Heading west on County Highway X, going toward the town of Menomonie and heading out of Chippewa Falls, there sits an old train bridge on the left-hand side of the road. There are so many of these bridges that are now abandoned or no longer used for railroad transportation. Unlike other forgotten railway bridges, this particular one is still used today. It was first constructed in 1917 with concrete arches and five deck plate girder main spans (DPG) and then rebuilt in 1998 with five brand-new DPG main spans. I will say, truthfully, there is definitely more than meets the eye to this structure.

On the chilled winter day of December 20, 1924, the Minneapolis Saint Paul and Sault Ste. Marie Railway, or the Soo Line, had a passenger train that was making its way over this now said to be ill-fated bridge. It was a clear icy day at approximately 12:24 in the afternoon when tragedy suddenly struck. On this single line, heading eastbound, train number two, which consisted of three mail and express cars, one baggage car, two coaches, one sleeping car and one café observation car, suddenly derailed and plunged over the bridge into the icy water below. In the official report, it was stated that the train was running about an hour late and traveling at about twenty-five miles per hour at the time of the accident. The rear trunk of the rear car derailed at the switch, which eventually swerved to the left, until it reached the very center of the bridge itself. One car broke loose from the other, and then it plummeted over the side, falling upside down into the water. The staff on board were not injured and also relayed that there was nothing they could have done to stop the accident. Later on, it was found there was a broken switch bolt that was the cause of the derailment. Eight individuals lost their lives that fated winter day, and seven more sustained severe injuries. There was a federal investigation later conducted, but the investigation found that it was indeed the broken switch bolt that was the sole cause of the derailment. Unfortunately for Harry Caldwell, the conductor, this news of the broken bolt did not reach him in time. According to *Haunted Chippewa Falls*, by Chris Wiener and Clarence Rice, it was stated Harry Caldwell was "a great man with a perfect record." Even though the fault was mechanical, Mr. Caldwell took the accident personally, blaming himself. No other news would have appeased him, in my opinion. It was reported he committed suicide by hanging himself off the very bridge where the derailment occurred. Others state his suicide took place in the general area near the tracks. Perhaps his ghost still lurks about one of these two areas.

Fishermen down by the water have reported that early in the morning they have seen people "coming out of the water." These entities then vanish before the fishermen's eyes. According to authors Wiener and Rice, they state that there was a photo taken shortly after the train wreck. If you look past the wreckage and people, there seems to be eight shadow people who cannot be accounted for. Ironically enough, that is the same number of people killed in the accident. To speculate, the shadows could be due to the old photograph and blurs in the photo causing this to appear. However, some believe these blurry shadow people are the ghosts of the victims who lost their lives back on that winter day in 1924.

Poor Harry Caldwell. If he wouldn't have been so overcome with his grief over the accident, he would have found out that the switch bolt became crystallized by the fifteen degrees below zero temperature and then snapped under the weight of the train. I often wonder if his spirit lurks about, perhaps still carrying the weight of the world on his shoulders. But he may not be the only person with cause to stick around. According to an online find I came across, there were reports at the scene of the accident that stated there were two bodies that had been spotted in the water after the coach took its deadly plunge. However, this could not be verified and was later discounted. I question if there really were two bodies that went unaccounted for. Are they still wandering around this area because they were never properly laid to rest? There is comfort that all was not lost that day though. There were two boys, Dayton Gonyea and Raymond Walthers, who were walking near the railroad when they heard steel against steel and then a loud crash followed by the sounds of something splashing into the water. Both of the boys ran to the center of the bridge, and Dayton Gonyea pulled out an extra pair of gloves, throwing them to two women who were down below in the water. The women had managed to crawl out of the car and started waving their hands for help. According to the Gonyea Family Genealogy website:

> Then, with Walthers at his heels, Gonyea ran half a mile down stream to a flat bottom skiff, rode back to the scene of the tragedy, and with Walthers and Wesley Cardinal, 10, helped seven of the victims from the freezing stream and battered car. The boys worked for half an hour before exhaustion forced them to relinquish their activities to townsmen and members of the fire department, which Gonyea had ordered a chum to call before he ran for the boat.

The "Old Train Bridge" in Chippewa Falls, 2011. *Photo courtesy of the Bells' personal collection.*

Seven people saved and eight deaths. To this day there is still probably energy that was created from the accident that lingers still, good and bad. Many of the victims, who either died or were severely injured, were on their way to see family for Christmas. This is a must-see if ever you are in Chippewa Falls, Wisconsin. While at the bridge, stop and stand in silence. Perhaps you will hear the screaming of the people in the icy water or the shouts of the boys who aided them so heroically that day. Look closer and maybe you will see the figure of the guilt-stricken conductor, swinging back and forth from one of the trestles of the bridge. Maybe, just maybe, this area is a bridge where the living and the dead coexist as one.

CHAPTER 4

A HAUNTINGLY COLD CASE

S ome of the greatest, spookiest stories are those of tales based on true events. The story of Mary Schlais has all the makings of a spine-tingling tale. Journeys usually end with an exciting conclusion, the feeling of completion, of moving on to the next adventure. But for twenty-five year old Mary, her journey ended in terror…and the ultimate betrayal.

After graduating from the University of Minnesota with honors in 1973, Mary Kathleen Schlais was ready to make her mark. Young, bright and accomplished, she had already seen so much of the world, traveling to Europe and also around most of the United States, many times hitchhiking her way through. She spoke German and Danish fluently and was beginning to learn Japanese as well. With a great passion for art, Mary started putting her work up in exhibits, where she showed off her sculptures, paintings and drawings. I have often wondered what sort of future she would have had. I think Mary would have gone on to do great things, maybe taken the world by storm with her talents. But that was never to be as her life was cut short much too soon.

In 1974, Mary was busy studying for her master's degree and also showing off her art. The independent young woman she was, it is speculated that in February of this same year, she decided to

Mary Schlais in Austria, early 1970s. *Photo courtesy of Chris Schlais.*

hitchhike to an art show in Chicago. In the 1970s, hitchhiking was more common and accepted, not as feared as it is today. But when Mary got as far as Elk Lake Dam in Dunn County, Wisconsin, she met with a deadly road block.

Mary decided to start what was to be her final journey on the morning of February 15, 1974. Her roommate, Judith Daniel, later told authorities she had left between 10:30 and 10:45 a.m. from their uptown Minneapolis apartment on foot. She wore a sign with the word "Madison" so she could make her way to Chicago obtaining rides from passerby. By 1:15 that afternoon, her body was found near the Elk Lake area, which is on the line between Eau Claire and Dunn County. This is where the mystery begins. The authorities ended up with the details of a man who was seen dumping her body into a snowy ditch on a dead-end road. A local resident (Denny Anderson) in the area saw a gold-colored compact car and what appeared to be two men arguing. After driving down the road farther, he decided to turn around and then realized this was no ordinary spat. He saw a woman's body in the ditch, and the white male with the gold car was gone. After running for help, authorities were on the scene. But it was too late: Mary Schlais was dead, having been stabbed about fifteen times with defensive wounds to her hands. When she was found, her body was still warm and there was a stocking cap found at the crime scene and also tire impressions were made. The odd thing was that Mary's coat and purse were nowhere to be found. After analysis, nothing came of the impressions or DNA from the hair found inside the stocking cap. Eight months after the murder, an anonymous person sent a letter to the crime lab that read, "Did you ever think man who found murdered girl at Elk Lake also put her there." Whether there was truth to this pointing of a finger or it was some sick, bored individual, we'll never know. This heinous crime happened over thirty years ago and remains a cold case. In May 1974, a new student art gallery at the University of Minnesota was dedicated in Mary's honor.

Mary was laid to rest in Champlin Cemetery located in Champlin, Minnesota. In 2009, her body was exhumed for further DNA research, but as of yet, there has been no other information to shed light on this tragedy. Family and friends of Mary still have fervent hope that her killer will be brought to justice. They will not let go and keep on fighting. It seems as though Mary hasn't let go either and is still trying to communicate from beyond the grave.

Several years ago, two men were down by Elk Creek Dam fishing. One of the men turned around to look behind him, then turned back to his fishing buddy and exclaimed, "There's a glowing white woman behind us." His friend did not turn his head and simply said, "I know, but I'm not turning around." Many have spun tales of seeing a woman by the side of the bridge along the lake, a vanishing hitchhiker or even a woman coming out of the water toward them. A woman by the name of Virginia Hendricks, who passed away in 1995, lived near the dam and would mention that in the fall of 1994, she received daily visits from a young blonde woman in her early twenties known only as "Mary." She would come to visit at the same time every morning and afternoon wearing the same outfit and would walk through the elderly lady's garden or tap on her window. I have read about people, sometimes elderly or others who are dying or going to die shortly, who communicate with the dead. It is often speculated that because that person's life is going to be ending, their senses are heightened and a spirit can somehow sense this and therefore perhaps latch onto that person, befriending them from the beyond. Whatever happened between Virginia and "Mary" is a fascinating, tender story. Perhaps all Mary wanted was to have someone to talk to. Maybe she cannot leave the area where her life was taken. Maybe she is trapped between realms and cannot or will not pass on until her death is avenged and her killer is brought to justice. In reviewing details of the murder, I have wondered if this was a crime of passion because she was killed the day after Valentine's Day. She was a beautiful, vibrant young lady who was alone and vulnerable in her travels. Dunn County detectives and also the family of Mary think that she knew her killer. If Mary's ghost or spirit *is* wandering around Elk Lake Dam, maybe she is trying to tell us something. This is indeed a fascinating concept for ghost lore. We have a location and also a horrible tragedy.

I myself have visited this place numerous times and always have a feeling of peace there. Just remember that by day you can take in all the beautiful scenery, but by night it is easy to become swallowed up in the darkness. Things never appear the same from day to night. If you decide to visit Elk Lake Dam and its infamous ghost, keep your wits about you. But don't worry; if Mary is indeed there, I think she is a peaceful ghost, one who has lost her way and cannot continue on until her murder is truly solved. If she is out there, perhaps all she wants is to communicate with someone, so she will have peace at last.

Back in 2009, my husband and I were very much into paranormal investigating. One of the first places we went to was "Mary of Elk Creek." Our eyes and ears played tricks on us, but I remember getting one EVP (electronic voice phenomenon) that was pretty inaudible. However, one incident left me chilled to the bone and made me practically jump out of my own skin. My husband, two friends and

Headshot of Mary Schlais, 1966. *Photo courtesy of Chris Schlais.*

I were standing down by the creek conducting EVPs. I was holding an EMF reader, which is a device that reads electromagnetic fields. Often times, ghosts or spirits feed off of energy to communicate or move items. As I was holding the EMF device, I asked Mary if she was present and if she could make the needle on the device spike. I said to my husband, "Hey, the needle moved. What's this mean?" He answered with a shocked look on his face, "That probably means she's standing right in front of you." I almost dropped the EMF reader! I couldn't believe that maybe, just maybe, she was communicating with me. All the times I had used the EMF device, nothing like this had ever happened and, I might add, hasn't happened since. I asked again, "Mary, was that you that made the needle move? Can you do that again?" Just like before, the needle moved, this time not as much. During this time we were also using what's called a Frank's

Box, which is a device that uses AM/FM radio stations, even stray stations that can pick up a spirit's voice on the frequency waves. The device scans channels constantly and what investigators listen for are words they can possibly put together after asking a question to the dead. Sometimes investigators use white noise or background noise to conduct EVP sessions. The Frank's Box or more popularly called the "Ghost Box" is still controversial. Some claim it's foolish, and we shouldn't read more into it, while others swear that it is a great tool for paranormal investigators to use. The night the EMF reader went off the charts, one of our friends was asking questions while listening to the Frank's Box. Right after the EMF incident, he started hearing an odd pulsating sound that he hadn't heard before. He then asked Mary if she was doing this. The pulsing got stronger. So he asked,

Elk Lake Dam, 2010. *Photo courtesy of the Bells' personal collection.*

"Mary, if this *is* you, can you make it stop?" It immediately stopped. He asked her to make it start again, and it did.

This location holds such a tragic event in its clutches, an event that may never be solved. As I write this part of the book, I realize that this year marked the thirty-ninth anniversary of this unsolved murder. There is one detective in Menomonie who has not forgotten and continues to look into the cold case. I myself have had the pleasure of being contacted by a family member of Mary's who has been very helpful. I know the family wants closure. Mary might want the same. This is not just another paranormal tale that's been spun or made up out of thin air, told by a campfire or used as an initiation for teenagers over the years. It is based on a *real* crime that happened. If you visit the dam and park, I ask that you please show courtesy to those who live in the area and to Mary's memory.

R.I.P. Mary Kathleen Schlais
1948–1974

CHAPTER 5

SCHOOL SPIRIT

T hroughout the United States, higher education is embraced and often times is the core of family tradition. The University of Wisconsin–Eau Claire is no different with its sprawling campus, lush green lawns and hundreds of students scattered about. According to the official college website:

> *UW–Eau Claire was founded in 1916 as the Eau Claire State Normal School, housed in a single building constructed on 12 acres of land. The institution evolved into a State Teachers College in 1927, the Wisconsin State College at Eau Claire in 1951 and attained university status in 1964. In 1971 the university, with other state-supported higher learning institutions, became a full partner in the new UW System and has continued to expand its mission of providing quality undergraduate programs in liberal arts and sciences, business, education, nursing, human sciences and services, and pre-professional programs.*

Generations of students have flocked through the massive doors and have eagerly embraced their futures. But perhaps some students have not. Along with the hustle and bustle, it seems as though there are some very "spirited" comings and goings of ghostly pupils as well.

THE DAVIES CENTER

The Davies Center is located on the UW–Eau Claire Campus. The following information was obtained from the uwec.edu website. Ground was broken for it on November 20, 1957. It was initially named the College Center, and the building was the first student center. It was built when the school was called the Wisconsin State College at Eau Claire. The construction cost $750,000 and was funded entirely by student fees and designed by the Eau Claire architectural firm Larson, Playter and Smith. When the building was finished in September 1959 and opened its doors, there were 1,078 students and 97 faculty members. In December1959, the College Center was named the Davies Center in memory of William R. Davies (1893–1959). Davies was the second president of the University of Wisconsin–Eau Claire. The Davies Center was also the first building on campus to be named after an individual. In 1964, it doubled in size, and expansions and updates were made to the building in 1976, 1982 and 1991.

In 2006, the UW System Board of Regents approved the student-initiated and funded redevelopment of the Davies Center. By 2009, it was made official that there would be a new student center built. The original Davies Center would then be torn down. I drove past what was left of the Davies shortly after it was demolished and remember just a pile of rubble standing in its place. It was sad to see it go, but a bigger, more modern building is now standing. The new building, which was designed by Kraemer Brothers, LLC out of Plain, Wisconsin, opened its doors July 30, 2012. The old site of the original Davies Center is now a sort of meditation garden/grounds for students.

The website ghostsofamerica.com had some information on the alleged activity at the old Davies Center. An individual who went by the name of "Jess" said, "Here late night workers have experienced an apparition of a man who appears to be a railroad worker. A scream coming from a stage when no one is in the theater (there is no back entrance either) or the lights in the theater turning off, and a little girl wanders around. A friend of mine thought she (the ghost child) must have been pulling her keys out of her back pocket over and over again until she asked her to stop since she needed to work." To clarify, the old Davies did have theaters. My husband and I attended a film festival there a couple years ago.

Now that the old center has been torn down, I wonder if there *are* ghosts still lurking about and whether they will remain rooted to this location, unable or unwilling to pass over.

KJER THEATRE

My first experience at the Kjer Theatre was memorable, just not the way you may think. When I was about fourteen or fifteen years old, I attended the musical *Fiddler on the Roof* with my mother. When I was in my early teens I was very active with local musical theater and was excited to see some of my friends in this musical on the Eau Claire college campus. Unfortunately, I was very sick with a horrible cold and really painful ear infection. But we had the tickets, and even though I wasn't feeling the greatest, I still wanted to go. All I really remember is trying to watch the show and every time I swallowed, my ear would pop and hurt so badly! I barely remembered the inside of the theater and just wanted to get home and crawl into bed. Years later, after learning it was reported to be haunted, I shudder just a bit. I wonder if I'm getting the chills from thinking of possible supernatural activity or from the memories of that painful earache.

On the University of Wisconsin–Eau Claire campus at the corner of Garfield Avenue and Park Avenue stands the Earl S. Kjer Theatre. The theater was built in 1951 and was first used in 1952. At this time, it was called the Little Theatre. According to the University of Wisconsin–Eau Claire website, "The groundbreaking ceremony for the Brewer Hall–Zorn Arena–Kjer Theatre complex was held on October 20, 1950. The cornerstone was laid on September 19, 1951 and full use of each unit of the complex was achieved in September 1952. In 1965, to honor faculty member, director of theater, and chair of the Department of Speech, the theater was named the Kjer Theatre, after Earl S. Kjer."

Earl S. Kjer was born on December 15, 1903, and taught drama and speech at the University of Wisconsin–Eau Claire. He married Vera M. Kjer (1908–2001) in New London. Mr. Kjer passed away on January 25, 1965, from acute myocardial infarction due to arterio-sclerotic coronary thrombosis at the age of sixty-one. Kjer was laid to rest at the Forest Hill Cemetery (a cemetery rumored to be haunted) in Eau Claire. Earl Kjer loved his job and loved the theater so much that perhaps he couldn't leave it behind in death.

According to local reports, Kjer has been seen sitting in his favorite seat of the theater and also been known to tamper with lights, props and curtains. Usually the ghostly activity occurs on or near the opening night of a show. Employees of the campus claim that Earl is famous there, and many students know of his ghost or spirit. At times when items go missing in the theater, some blame it on Earl. When the door rattles or the doorknob shakes, Earl did it. A custodian for the theater claimed that sometimes the pipes make noises but added that he doesn't believe in ghosts. Others talk about Kjer having a favorite seat, one that he sat in for every production. Now when anyone sits in that seat, some have reported to have heard the ghost yell at them in anger. Sometimes individuals feel a presence, and it really scares them.

I found an article called, "Kjer to Join Me?" from 2006 on the *Spectator* online, the official newspaper for the University of Wisconsin–Eau Claire. A student who at the time was a sophomore named Eddie Neve talked about how he had heard of the rumors and kept waiting, watching for

The Kjer Theater, 2012. *Photo courtesy of the Bells' personal collection.*

anything to happen. Later that same year, he became a believer. He was in the spring production of *Bat Boy*, and one night after the show, he was one of the last to finish taking off his theatrical makeup. He went onto the stage and saw a side door was ajar, as if someone had just pushed it open. As he started to leave, he looked back one last time and, to his shock, saw the door slowly close by itself. The article went on to state, "'I knew nobody was there so I was freaked,' he said. 'Now I won't go in there if it's dark and I'm by myself.'"

So there you have it. Over the years, equipment has continuously been tampered with, students and faculty have felt a presence in the empty theater when no one is there and others just simply say, "Earl did it."

KATHERINE-THOMAS RESIDENCE HALL

The Katherine-Thomas residence hall supposedly has activity of its own, and the spirit(s) there are not exactly friendly.

According to a person by the name of Jess, "The other building is Katherine-Thomas residence hall where a room on the first floor is haunted by a red-headed angry girl in a white nightgown. She has been known to throw things across the room. On upper floors people have spotted an old woman who wanders the halls. When they ask her who she's looking for she disappears." The last part of lore this individual spoke of was phantom heels clicking along the hallways. This person said she know someone who lived in the building and they have also heard stories from friends of friends as well.

An angry little spirit girl and the restless ghost of an elderly woman. Perhaps the young girl and the elderly woman are grandmother and granddaughter and are eternally in search of each other?

GOVERNOR'S HALL

I recently found information from the website Ghostsofamerica.com regarding the Governor's Hall. Some have reportedly seen the spirit of a man in a particular room where it is said he took his life years ago. Some say that he wears a white hospital gown or robe that has the Sacred Heart Hospital logo on it. Rumors have circulated that this young man had a horrible incurable disease and he could not cope with the tragic illness. As a result, he committed suicide and has never left the room where he drew his last breath. Some individuals report that the encounters have not been malicious, but others talk about his wild mood swings and the fear they felt of being harmed. According to Thomas, the person who wrote the article, the last sighting was back in 2006.

LITTLE NIAGRA

Little Niagra is a creek that empties into the Chippewa River and is right in front of the University of Wisconsin–Eau Claire's campus. Students come and go, people walk their dogs and some may even go down by the creek and put their toes in the water. I wonder how many realize this was the very site of two eerie deaths.

I found an online column on the Volume One website written by Chad Lewis. There was a particular article that caught my attention called, "Drowned in Chippewa May 16, 1905." It was originally published in the *Eau Claire Leader Telegram* and weaves a very tragic tale.

The beginning of the article reads, "Such is supposed to have been the fate of Fred Kenney, aged 11. Coincidence in Tragedy. Arthur, a brother of Fred, was drowned near the same locality." This eleven-year-old boy drowned in just about the same spot where his brother Arthur had drowned ten years prior. Freddie Kenney was the son of Patrick Kenney and met the same *exact* fate as his brother. A schoolmate of Freddie's, Roy Hunner, told Mr. Kenney that his little boy had disappeared. According to Roy, he and Freddie had gone down to Little Niagra right after school the day before in the afternoon. Roy wanted to go up the hill and pick flowers, but Freddie didn't want to go. Roy left him behind and went to pick flowers by himself. After some time had passed, Roy came back to the spot where he left Freddie and found the boy's shoes and socks on the riverbank not far from the water. However, there were absolutely no signs of young Freddie. His companion became very frightened and ran back to town to spread the word that his friend had gone missing. Unfortunately, it was too late at night to start a search team, and some thought perhaps Freddie had gathered his belongings and was on his way home already. But that next morning, he didn't come home and his father gathered some of his friends and went down to the river to drag it. They too found Freddie's shoes and socks on the riverbank with no signs of the boy nearby.

According to Lewis, it was thought that little Freddie was pulled to his watery grave in the same exact spot his brother met the same fate ten years earlier. He assumed that the boys were both playing at their favorite watering hole and accidentally drowned. It wasn't until he read the entire article that he realized Fred was just an infant at the time of his brother's death, which would make it impossible that they would have both swam at this very location together. The article itself gave very little information on Freddie's brother's drowning, but after digging a bit, Lewis found that this case was even odder than he originally had thought. Not only did Freddie drown in the same location as his brother Arthur, but they were both the same age at the time of their deaths. You see, ten years prior to little Freddie's drowning, his older brother Arthur was down by the river with friends and decided to test his skill by walking out on the jammed logs that were crossing the river. None of his friends were as daring as he, so they just sat back and watched him from the safety of the riverbank. Arthur lost his balance and was swept away down the river. A local fisherman saw the entire accident and dove in after the boy but was too late: Arthur was already gone.

At the time of the *Leader* article regarding young Freddie's disappearance, his family was holding out hope that he would be found alive. Unfortunately, on June 5, his lifeless body was found near Caryville, Wisconsin. Ironically, Caryville is a popular place for ghost lore and so many are drawn to this area yearly. Perhaps little Freddie's spirit has joined the other restless dead in that area.

If you find yourself in the city of Eau Claire, venture on down to the college campus. There's so much activity and energy from all the students and faculty that you may not notice the shadow staring at you from an upper window of the Katherine-Thomas Hall. Step inside the Kjer Theater and be on the lookout for old Mr. Kjer himself. Just make sure you don't occupy his special seat, otherwise you may find yourself being reprimanded by a ghost. But don't let it get you down. Come now, where's your school "spirit"?

CHAPTER 6

THE ASYLUM HILL

A book about haunted locations wouldn't be complete without an old asylum to add to the mix. Even though the Eau Claire Asylum no longer stands today, there have been reports from local residents who claim that some restless spirits have stayed behind.

Back in the early fall of 1999, a group of four friends were hanging out at "the hill," as they called it. The "hill" is the former site of where the Eau Claire Asylum and Poor Farm were located. The site where the large asylum stood was up a slope along the south side of Truax (east across North Clairemont Avenue) and is more or less between Old Orchard Road and County Farm Road. I found a site online that stated the former physical address would have been 1405 Truax Boulevard. While the friends were there, one of them decided to leave and go pick up his brother so he could join them as well. That's when the creepy encounter happened. As the group of now three stood around talking, they heard someone or some*thing* run up behind them quickly within about ten feet of where they were, but when they turned around, thinking it was one of their friends playing a trick on them, there was no one there. The group disbanded abruptly and ran.

Another incident happened with a different set of friends. It was December of 2000, and four friends were up at the eerie hill. As they all started into the woods to obtain shelter from the chill winter wind, they heard the sounds of footsteps upon gravel and sounds of feet kicking at or crunching leaves. They all looked at each other a bit stumped because it didn't make sense to be hearing those sounds. It was wintertime, and there were many inches of snow on the ground. Just like the first group of friends, they all ran as fast as they could from the mysterious hill.

The Eau Claire County Asylum was designed by architect C.L. Brown and built in 1900, and the original cost, including a farm of 466 acres, the building and all the equipment, came to $135,284. It opened its doors for residents in 1901. When this site and the farm were bought for the purpose to build the asylum, the grounds were laid out by F.W. Woodward. Like many institutions and poor farms, some of the residents who resided there were able to work on the farm and grow their own food. The women would then tend to making clothing and household chores. In 1913, the Eau Claire County Asylum housed 168 people, with 71 from Eau Claire County. The poor farm itself was originally located about four miles southeast of Eau Claire but was later sold, and 31 acres of ground was purchased to the west for $36,000 in 1928 and was then used as the actual asylum farm, which stood right next to the institution. In 1913, the poor farm itself housed 14 residents.

By 1943, old-age pensions had reduced the number of residents from fifty-six down to only nineteen. A fellow by the name of John Lindner suggested abandoning the home and pensioning the residents as the county was operating at a deficit. E.S. Leverich was superintendent at the time, and in 1949, the home was leased to the Incani family to run. The asylum was demolished circa 1984, according to a more recent *Eau Claire Leader* article.

Like many other asylums and poor farms, there were also cemeteries either on the grounds or located about a mile or so away. What used to be called the Asylum Cemetery is now called the Eau Claire County Old Orchard Cemetery. In 2007, the county almost renamed it the Pauper's Cemetery, but at the closing of Eau Claire's 130th birthday, it was voted

The Eau Claire Asylum, circa early 1900s. *Photo courtesy of the Eau Claire Landmarks Commission.*

by the board to keep the name of the Old Orchard Cemetery. A large marker was erected in the front and center of the cemetery grounds with the name and dedication to all who were buried there. The majority of these markers actually have names and dates engraved upon them. However, there are several that say Jane or John Doe, as well as unknown markers as well. There are approximately 160 graves in this once-forgotten graveyard.

Old asylums and poor farms are, for the most part, a thing of the past. Many of them have been torn down or revamped for other use. The Eau Claire County Asylum and poor farm are a perfect example of history that is long gone but not forgotten. At least, it hasn't been forgotten by those groups of friends who had peculiar experiences on what they had nicknamed "the hill." What stands today is an old, torn-up parking lot used by nurses and staff. There is now woods and a newer park where everything used to be back at the turn of the century.

Perhaps the dead still live on these grounds, or maybe they have moved on to another world or realm. Take a trip over to "the hill" sometime, and you just might have an adventure of your own to tell.

CHAPTER 7

THE CASTLE

I love the Elk Mound Tower; everything from the medieval looking structure to the majestic scenery when standing at the very top is so surreal. I remember seeing it from afar several years ago and never once thought it could be haunted.

The Elk Mound Tower or the "Overlook Tower" is located in the town of Elk Mound, Wisconsin. It is the second-highest hill in the state of Wisconsin and was named Mound Hill Park by several local residents. Mound Hill was thought to have been used by the Sioux and Chippewa Indians as a look-out spot. From either close up or far away, it appears like a small castle or building from the medieval world of Camelot. This two-story tower was actually built as a memorial for the Deceased Rural Letter Carriers of Dunn County, according to the exact wording on the marker itself, and is believed to be the only one of its kind in the nation.

In 1924, Paul Kreck built Highway 12, and in 1926, he put up a flagpole where the tower is now located. Earl Hansen and Leon Cartwright, who were owners of farms north of the hill, built the first dirt road that led up to the tower, sometime after the year 1924. The hill and park were deeded to the Village and County by Louis and Marie Nelson in 1933. In 1934, rural letter carriers of Dunn County planted a tree on the top of the mound, also placing a plaque with an inscription of dedication on it that read, "Deceased Rural Letter Carriers of Dunn County." Soil was taken from *every* carrier's route and placed around the tree. On June 8, 1937, the Dunn County board voted on and accepted the park and three acres surrounding it as a county park. This same year, the county, along with the Works Progress Administration aid, constructed an observation tower or "the castle" as others like to call it. This tower was twenty-five feet in height, and the stones used for the structure came from the Downsville stone quarry. The additional stones and material came from a dismantled livery stable in the nearby village. There was a dedication ceremony held on Friday, November 11, 1938, and roll call of deceased rural letter carriers was sealed in a granite marker atop the hill next to the tower.

The county eventually turned Mound Hill Park back to the village of Elk Mound, and it was then closed in 1987 due to liability and safety concerns with the steep road. Later, seniors from the Elk Mound High School worked for six years to improve and revamp the tower for a part of their community service projects. The dirt road was paved, new guard rails were put in and a general clean-up of the area was done as well. In 1994, there was a rededication ceremony at the park. Because of continuous support, the village was able to erect a new flag pole on November 11, 2002, and then lighting was added to it on November 11, 2003. I really like how they always stuck with the date of November 11 since the first dedication in 1938.

Apart from a dedicated plaque and soil around the tree on the hill, there is also a legend of a fire-breathing dragon buried under the mound, directly under the tower. There has also been a report of a person falling to his death from the tower back in the 1980s when it was closed to the public prior to renovations. Now some say the restless spirit of the victim haunts the grounds. People have reported feeling nauseated while at the tower and also hearing screams, howling and laughter at times as well. I even came across a website that spoke of hearing children's laughter and sounds of playing in the woods, but no one was there. Visions of strange mists have been seen, and some individuals have seen odd lights in or around the tower at night from the road. Others say if you walk up the stairs in the tower, you might hear footsteps behind you, but when you turn around no one will be there. Due to all the odd occurrences, the road to the tower was blocked off for many years.

The real reason the road was blocked off was the maintenance that was needed for safety purposes. There has never been proof of the existence of a buried dragon, and according to investigators Chad Lewis and Terry Fisk, feelings of nausea while in the tower could be from someone experiencing vertigo. There has also never been any concrete proof of an accidental or suicidal death on or around the tower.

But I hope this doesn't derail anyone from visiting. This park has so much to offer other than just ghost lore. It's a piece of history and has amazing panoramic views of Elk Mound and beyond. Believe me, you can get some pretty great photos off your digital camera wherever you point it. I have often thought of the Native Americans and how they utilized the hill years ago. Perhaps there is an old burial ground beneath the tower instead of a dragon.

When I look at the tower today, I can't believe that it used to have screened-in windows, doors, a cookstove, picnic tables and a fireplace. What remains now is basically the shell of what used to be. But at least it has been maintained and is still around for tourists and locals to visit and enjoy. The tower is currently open from May 1 through October 31 and is then closed every winter. In my opinion, take the opportunity and go check it out on Halloween!

CHAPTER 8

THE BLOOMER MASSACRE

I have oftentimes heard the saying "too close to home." Never in a million years would I ever truly believe this statement, but after discovering the story of several horrific murders, I can honestly say that I am now a believer and think that anything can happen anywhere and anytime. I want to take you back to the day of November 16, 1981 (ironically, that was my second birthday). There is an RV business called Willie's Mobile Home Park & Trailer Sales, which has a house near it, and then just down the street, there is a trailer park. It's located outside of Bloomer, Wisconsin, which is the start of what is called "the Northwoods." This trailer park and RV center are located off of Highway 64 and conveniently right off of the main Highway 53. It was a normal autumn day in the rural farming community of Bloomer. I know this town well because I lived there for so long; in fact, I lived with my parents only a couple miles away from this very RV business for about ten years. I spent time at Willie's when my grandparents visited, parking their RV at the campgrounds. A crime like the one I am about to share with you is not the norm for the tiny town of Bloomer. It's a small town with hardly any violence or crime. Children can run around with their friends at night. Many residents leave doors unlocked, and people wave at one another even if they don't know each other. One of the most popular pastimes is jump-roping, and the town is called "the Rope Jumping Capital of the World." For all these idyllic details and more, no one could believe what happened that fateful fall day in November 1981.

As the unsuspecting individuals inside the recreation vehicle sales office at the nearby trailer park were going about their daily business, they didn't notice the man stepping inside the office with a shotgun. As the shots rang out, no one for miles seemed to pay any attention to the blasts because of the deer hunters out in the nearby woods conducting target practice for deer season. A short time later, a woman stood inside her home, perhaps doing the dishes or laundry. Maybe she turned after hearing the movement or a strange sound just outside the house. Perhaps she had this sick feeling in the pit of her stomach that something was horribly wrong. It didn't matter. She was already marked for death.

Norm Fox, a friend of the Dietsche family, walked into the sales office and met with the ultimate horror. His eyes beheld the slain victims of sixty-two-year-old Wilbur Dietsche; his twenty-two-year-old son, Arden; and twenty-two-year-old employee Loren Stolt. His blood turning ice cold, he lunged for the nearest phone, his hands shaking, and called the local police department to tell them of this horrifying scene. Norm's wife went on to later state, "Norm got there before the police got up there. That never left him. He was traumatized from that day on."

After the sheriff's department arrived, they identified all three victims and then had to make a very difficult visit to Wilbur's sixty-five-year-old wife, Lenora, at home. However, when they knocked, there was no answer. They knocked again, but still no answer. They then walked in and found poor Lenora dead on the floor in a pool of blood. Now there were four deaths and even more confusion. People in the trailer park court heard the news quickly and were peeking out their windows to see their very own trailer court being roped off as the scene of a crime. Most of them left that very night and did not return until the next day for fear that the monster who committed these slayings was still on the loose and in the general area. "They were highly respected. They were good people," said Police Chief Parkhurst, regarding the Dietsche family. He also stated, "Knowing those people, I would have to say that any disputes they might have had with anybody would have been resolved in a mild, quiet way." No one could fathom why this family or their employee Loren Stolt would meet such a horrible fate. Who would commit such a heinous act, and in this neck of the woods? Law enforcement went on to report that all the victims were shot in the head and that the motive for the killings was not robbery. They said that billfolds carried by the men were not tampered with, including Wilbur Dietsche's, which contained a substantial amount of money. A scan of the office showed nothing was out of place. The Dietsche family were longtime residents of the Bloomer area and had operated the trailer park for about fifteen years. They were considered highly respected businesspeople and did not seem to have any enemies whatsoever. Their son, Arden, was an honor student at Bloomer High School and a spring graduate of the University of Minnesota. He then went on to join his family and was a business partner. So why would this respected, well-loved, God-fearing family meet with such a gruesome end?

The events of this day in 1981 were a blur for so many, but what happened the next day added to the ever-growing questions. On November 17, a resident of the mobile home park, twenty-nine-year-old Roger Johnson, shot himself to death as the Chippewa County Sheriff's Department closed in on him. They got word of Johnson and wanted to question him as a suspect in the murders of the day prior. He did not want to speak with them. Instead, he drove out to a stretch of countryside, pulled over and got out of his vehicle, shotgun in hand. He then walked onto the farmland of the Pecha family and proceeded to take his own life by shooting himself. Is it because he was guilty as charged? Or perhaps it was the fear of being convicted and going to prison an innocent man.

"We feel bad enough without all those details. We feel sorry for everyone that this had to happen," stated Johnson's father, Ervin

Willie's RV Center in Bloomer, 2012. *Photo courtesy of the Bells' personal collection.*

Johnson. "Roger never said anything about any problems," said another relative. "It's not like him to do it." He was called a "bully," a "kook" and "weirdo." He was a big man, six foot one and weighing about 240 pounds. He carried a cane that he seldom used and would sometimes tell people he was wounded in Vietnam. Because of the scars on his legs, many believed him. Yes, there was definitely something off about Roger Johnson. The scars on his legs came from a series of operations, not from serving his country. In fact, he never was in Vietnam or served at all. Many at the trailer court where he lived started complaining about him the summer before the murders took place. That summer, a woman by the name of Joan Mitchell said that Johnson called her and said he had her two daughters in his home and that he wanted her to stay away. She then went over to search, peering in the windows but couldn't see a thing. Frantic, she continued her search for her two daughters and eventually found them playing at a neighbor's house. Mitchell called police, but they had nothing to formally charge Roger with. Another individual said he had been told Johnson would many times tell children to stay away from his trailer because he had strange things inside and that he heard voices at times when no one was there. There were also rumors that he had a long arrest record, but all that was found were a couple of disorderly conduct arrests. There were rumors that Wilbur Dietsche had served Johnson with an eviction notice, but that was never proven. Many residents of the park claimed that Lenora Dietsche had told Roger Johnson to leave the trailer park for good. Still, there really was no concrete reason for Johnson to kill. "We really don't have a motive," said the sheriff. "He just flaked out. For some reason, he just had it in for them. He thought they were against him." Well, it sounds to me like good ol' Roger Johnson was a force to be reckoned with. Take consuming rage and apply a possible mental disorder such as paranoid schizophrenia to the mix, and this was a deadly cocktail to be sure. Only Roger wasn't going to let the cops have the last word. He wanted to remain silent...forever. You see, that day he took his life, the police were trying to catch up with him to ask a few questions. All those questions about if and why were to remain unanswered. If Roger Johnson did commit this truly horrible crime, he took his secrets and possibly confession to the grave. But dead men just might tell tales...

I was lurking around on the Unexplained Research website and came across some members on the board who were talking about the "Bloomer Massacre," as it is now referred to. One person said:

> Things didn't start happening till about five months ago. My kids and I have heard a female voice saying "help me" which has happened about seven times in the last few months. But last Friday was too much when my oldest called me at work and said that a lady's voice had said her name right in her ear while she was in the kitchen making a drink and her other two sisters were outside playing

and there was no one else in the trailer. I really got concerned tonight when we came home and my youngest child's bedroom had been re-arranged. I'm unsure as to what I should do! This has become really unnerving as of late. I'm unsure if this has to do with the murders that happened nearby or if it is something that's attached to my trailer or maybe the land. But right now I just want it to go away because it's scaring my kids.

This individual didn't know what to do and wanted to smudge her trailer (basically an action to ward off spirits), but she did not want to possibly heighten the problem and make things worse. She went on to say that she has also felt the presence of a cat. The family had felt something furry rubbing against their legs, but nothing was there. She then went on to say, "Recently I found out that my neighbors buried their dead kittens where my trailer now sits." That's just eerie and could shed some light on the furry little spirits pawing at them for attention. According to this member on the forum who goes by the name "Sixthsense," "Things have started to pick up here. My youngest has now seen an apparition of a young girl and dishes in the sink have started rattling in the kitchen. I talked with my neighbors tonight and they said they have been experiencing weird things too... something or someone pounding on the side of their trailer." Could it be the angry spirit of Roger Johnson himself? Then there is the odd smell of what seems like sulfur burning. She had a repairman look at the gas stove, but it was deemed just fine, so now the family is at a loss. Should they move out or learn to live with these disturbances?

Another member on the same board who goes by the name "lidia" reported:

I have lived in the trailer park since 1998. Do I think things go on here...possibly. I have had banging on my trailer at night, knocking on my door, running up and down my steps, then when I check outside there is nothing. My mom also lived here for awhile and she is very open to the paranormal. She also had things happen to her. I do have to say that I would never live in the lot where the murderer lived. One of the girls that used to live there used to have a lot of banging, running up and down her steps and heard other things inside her home. She moved out because of it.

Many other residents of this cursed trailer park have experienced the strange banging on the sides of their mobile homes and also have reported choking or wheezing sounds as if someone is being strangled. There is also the mysterious female entity asking for people to help her. Could this ghostly wail be that of Mrs. Dietsche crying out for help to anyone who can hear her? Maybe she is a spirit who, night after night, experiences the same events from November 16, when her life ended so violently. So many supernatural stories are spun from a heinous event like this. I wonder if the victims of that day still cannot rest because the murderer, whether it was Johnson himself or someone else, was never truly brought to justice. And the spirit of Roger Johnson may still walk among us, refuting his part in the murders and wanting to pronounce his innocence. Or perhaps he is just as evil in death as he was in life.

Let's go back again to November 1981. A steady stream of cars had pulled in front of Olson's Funeral Home. Three caskets inside held the bodies of Wilbur; his wife, Lenora; and young son Arden. A long black hearse pulled up just outside of St. Paul's Lutheran Church. Inside there was a silver blue casket that contained the body of Loren Stolt. Venture out forty miles to the north in the town of Rice Lake as funeral services were being prepared for Roger Johnson. Three tragic funerals all possibly connected to one another. Now the souls of the Dietsche family can be visited in the Auburn Cemetery. This country graveyard is the final resting place for many souls. Perhaps this cemetery is haunted, but just in the memories of visitors who come to honor the Dietsche family whose lives were cut short about thirty years ago.

As for the final resting place of Roger Johnson, I'm not sure. However, if ever you are in the Rice Lake area and decide to venture through the city cemetery, pay close attention and you just may find his grave. Be careful though: in life he did not like visitors, especially children at his trailer, and he may not want visitors at his grave site either!

In memoriam of:

Wilbur Dietsche, Lenora Dietsche, Arden Dietsche, Loren Stolt and Roger Johnson
May your souls rest in peace.

CHAPTER **9**

FRIGHT FACTORY

Ilove old factories and warehouses. They have that rustic, edgy appeal, and for any spook hunter or paranormal investigator, it's a dream location to explore. Located at 600 Wisconsin Street in Eau Claire, you will find a set of sprawling buildings. This is the site of the former Uniroyal Tire Factory that dominated this industrial section of Eau Claire back in the 1920s. With so much history, records of unusual phenomenon were long overdue.

The United States Rubber Company was originally founded in Naugatuck, Connecticut, in 1892. It was one of the original twelve stocks in the Dow Jones Industrial Average and became Uniroyal Inc. in 1961. Then in 1990, Uniroyal was bought by a France-based tire maker called Michelin. In effort to increase the share of automobile tires, in 1931, the U.S. Rubber Company bought a substantial portion of the Gillette Safety Tire Company. This company was founded in 1916 by Raymond B. Gillette, and its primary manufacturing plant was located in, yes, you guessed it…Eau Claire, Wisconsin! The plant held substantial contracts with the General Motors Corporation, and with the addition of U.S. Rubber products, it became one of the world's largest suppliers of original equipment tires.

In 1940, U.S. Rubber purchased the rest of the Gillette Company and began to expand and modernize the Eau Claire factory. As a result, production was increased greatly. During World War II, the rubber factories were devoted to production of war goods and produced military truck and airplane tires, as well as the canvas-top, rubber-soled jungle boots for soldiers and marines serving in tropical environments. By December 1943, the need for tires started to outweigh the need for ammunition. U.S. Rubber repurchased the plant from the government for over $1 million and converted it back to synthetic rubber tire production. At this point in time, the company started to expand and modernized itself, which lasted through 1951. When it ended, the Eau Claire plant was the fifth-largest tire facility in the United States. Then in 1965, the plant expanded yet again to produce tires for construction machinery, and for many years it was the largest private employer of Eau Claire and the second-largest in Chippewa Falls before it was closed in January 1991. The Michelin Group completely shut down the factory in Eau Claire, eliminating 1,350 jobs.

Now I'm sure that with such a large factory, there may have been accidental deaths. To this day, I haven't found anything substantial as to any worker deaths. Then again, the energy this building gives off lives on. The building stood empty for a short time and now is utilized for local offices and storefronts. The old factory is now called the Banbury Place, and the majority of buildings are still in use. One of the buildings was revamped and now has industrialized studio apartments. This is a concept I love to see: old buildings being utilized and not torn down or left to fall apart. Though perhaps with all the construction and revamping, something more than dust and dirt came to the surface.

According to investigators Terry Fisk and Chad Lewis, building number 13 is very unlucky indeed. Rumor has it that an electrician was accidentally electrocuted while working late one night on an air conditioning unit. His horribly burnt body was found the following week. Stories of workers falling into machinery and being crushed to death have been spoken of with macabre curiosity. There were reports of a major fire in one of the buildings resulting in a death. Building number 4 is now chained completely shut, and the inside is littered with dozens of rats. There are also reports of a maze of underground tunnels that connect to the buildings. Sometimes homeless people use them as short-term homes. Another bit of lore talks about one of the buildings being a shoe factory at one point in time. For some reason, it was shut down in mid-production and the equipment and other belongings were left behind. There were partially assembled shoes, pieces of rubber and open bottles of glue that still sit there today. It was almost as if the workers were evacuated from the building, never to return. One rumor is that this shoe company moved to nearby Chippewa Falls and is now the Red Wing Shoe Company

There is also a disc jockey by the last name of Snider who rented space and had a radio show at the Banbury Place. He believes he encountered the person haunting the building. On two different occasions, more than one person had seen this ghost in Snider's studio. A former disc jockey reported seeing a man with a red shirt looking through a window. Snider was the only other person in that building besides the DJ, and he had on a black shirt that day. The ghost with the red shirt appeared very suddenly and also came right through the window.

I also have a personal story to share. I have a friend whom I have known for years that used to work in one of the offices doing secretarial work. This was around the year 1999 or 2000. I worked nearby so used to stop in and visit with her when work was slow for her. She told me a story that her boss had told her about a man who worked in the factory back when it was Uniroyal Tire. They were pouring fresh cement in one of the halls, and the man fell in and was buried in the cement. They never retrieved his body. Now when I walk around, I always wonder if the man's body is right beneath my feet—if the story is true, that is.

Lewis and Fisk were able to find more information on the electrician who was killed. However, it was not an electrician but a tenant who died of an accidental electrocution while growing marijuana plants. He was trying to hook up an air conditioner for temperature control when the accident occurred. His body wasn't found until two weeks later. There has never been any further proof of a disastrous fire and also no further information of the Red Wing Shoe Factory. However the Mason Shoe Factory is located in Chippewa Falls but was never located in Eau Claire or at the Banbury Place.

Even though there were accounts that were later discounted, that doesn't stop the reports flooding in from different individuals who have had experiences. Some say since the untimely death in building 13, many hear strange sounds like moans, screams and the hum of an old air-conditioning unit. In building number 4, many have experienced an eerie unseen presence. Others have relayed seeing strange figures and shadows down in the tunnels or in the basements. I found a couple of odd accounts on the Internet. One was from around 2002 when a mother and daughter and her friend were driving to visit a family member. They got lost and stopped in front of building B. They knew it was the old factory that had been abandoned but had not heard about any of the supernatural tales. Their headlights were on the building, and the mother was looking down at the map for directions. Then her daughter's friend said, "Look at that guy in the window, that's kinda creepy…he's staring at us." She looked up and saw a man in a red and black plaid shirt looking out from the second-story window. She shrugged this off, thinking that perhaps he was a janitor or security guard, even though there were no lights on in the building and they saw no flashlight or any other form of light. When they finally arrived at their relative's house, they told her where they stopped, and she laughed, saying it was rumored to be haunted. They then told her what they saw. Another account is a bit comical and talks about a person eating a tootsie roll outside of one of the buildings at the old factory. She was looking at the "scary swan statue," which was an art project made from the garbage found in the Mississippi River that is perched in front of one of the old buildings. This person was looking at the statue of the swan and noticed that the tootsie roll she had been chewing was gone. The girl proclaimed she did not spit it out or swallow it.

Hungry ghosts? Vengeful spirits? Or maybe just a bunch of tall tales about an important piece of Eau Claire's history. The old sprawling factory looks quite dominating, with its clusters of large brick buildings. Some of it still looks abandoned and is used only for storage. But most of this old factory is in use and inhabited by the living day in and day out. Take a walk inside during business hours and see for yourself. Perhaps you will hear the blood-curdling screams of the poor man who was electrocuted or hear the tiny pitter-patter of mice scurrying about. Walking inside there is history everywhere you turn. There are large remnants of tires and other objects on display and pictures of the old factory hanging on the walls. Even looking down at your feet as you walk around, you can still see the concrete and cracks where tire workers walked so many years ago. Keep following in their tracks and you never know what you might find…

CHAPTER 10

PHANTOMS OF THE OPERA

I must admit, this is one landmark that I wish I could have seen. The Grand Opera House in Eau Claire was majestic and beautiful but unfortunately leveled many years ago.

The opera house project was finally full speed ahead three years after the first plans were made many years ago. The land was purchased, and it was announced the opera house would be standing in six months' time. Exactly six months later, there was an opera house! The Grand Opera House was bounded by Barstow, Main and River (now Graham) Streets. It stood on the west side of Barstow Street and was the second building south of Main Street. Land was cleared, and the excavating began in April 1883. I found an online article extracted from the *Eau Claire Leader Telegram* called "Special Publication, The Chippewa Valley and Beyond," published in 1976. According to the writer, Wayne Wolfert from the University of Wisconsin–Eau Claire Department of Speech, "By June walls were enclosing the building and timbers and roof trusses were at the site. The trusses measuring 72 by 11 feet and weighing more than a ton each, presented construction crews difficulties in raising them to the top of the more than four story support timbers, just as the lowering posed a problem for the wrecher (*sic*) 55 years later, in 1938." Vents were installed on the roof of the auditorium as well as the stage roof. A large chandelier, fourteen feet in diameter and twelve feet in height, hung over the audience. There were about 1,300 seats, and by mid-September, the wood and plasterwork was just about complete. The stage itself was thirty-five by seventy feet, and there were fourteen dressing rooms.

According to Wolfert:

> *The audience was as large as it was select. Wealth and fashion showed in the boxes and dress circle, presenting a display of elegant costumes worthy of any metropolis in America. In the parquette and balcony were the substantial citizens, who came to hear, not be seen. The auditorium when filled with people, still presented as it always did, the appearance of vast height which took away, in some degree, from the impression of the area. Today, those who witnessed a performance in the Grand Opera House speak fondly of the charming interior and especially of the pair of gracefully curved stairs at the rear of the orchestra which led to the balcony.*

A few of the performers who graced the stage were William Gillette, Pat Rooney, Gus Williams and John L. Sullivan. The theater was closed during the summer because of the heat and baseball season, which had become very popular.

The opera house was flooded by the Chippewa River and, in January 1884, was finally recovered after Barstow Street had been under eight feet of water. In 1892, after being foreclosed, the theater was sold by the sheriff to Delos R. Moon and remained in the Moon family for the rest of its existence. The opera house was also used for motion picture films starting in 1897 like many theaters during that era. The Edison Vitascope cast its "magic shadows on a sheet" hung on the stage of the opera house. I tell you, if I could have been a fly on the wall in that theater then, I bet it would have been quite the show!

During World War I, motion pictures started to slow. The year 1918 was the poorest year for theater in the forty-five-year history of the Grand Opera House. Also there was the Spanish influenza epidemic. Then in 1923, the Grand closed for the summer, which was the first time it closed

The Eau Claire Opera House, circa late 1800s. *Photo courtesy of the Eau Claire Landmarks Commission.*

since it was had been utilized for motion pictures. In 1924, the theater was leased by United Theaters but, because of the decline, was dropped six months later. Eventually, the Minneapolis Company took over all Eau Claire theaters, and the glorious Grand Opera House went dark, pretty much for good. From 1929 to 1930, the seasons started out well and with much promise. But after that, the theater couldn't hold on any longer and shut its doors. In 1938, the Grand Opera House was demolished. In the aftermath of the dust and debris, it seems as though some spirits still lurk about.

After the opera house was leveled, the Montgomery Ward Store occupied the site. There is now currently an office building where the opera house used to stand. The city of Eau Claire has paid homage to the old theater because the building still says "Opera House" on the outside, and in the front there is a plaque with a picture and information about the former site and theater. Now on the top floor of the building is a call center where it is said the location of the break room would have been the area that the actors would change costumes and do their makeup. It is also said that a few actors died in this same area. Employees of the call center have reported that late at night, doors to the break room shut by themselves, and the chairs will move by some unseen force. There have also been sightings of two elderly people who watch the workers and stand off in the corners, keeping to themselves. Could this ghostly couple be from the stage, or perhaps patrons of the arts who in life enjoyed coming to the theater so much they could not leave after they passed away? Maybe the spirits are trapped here and even though the opera house was leveled so many years ago, they linger still. I wonder if the spirits are angry that their theater is gone.

If you want to take a look at the former site of the Grand Opera House for yourself, all you have to do is walk downtown along Barstow and you will find it on the corner. The building is now being utilized as several businesses, along with the call center on the top floor. If you get the chance to get inside, walk up and down the halls and see if you find or feel anything out of the ordinary. Perhaps you will come face to face with one of the phantoms of the opera!

CHAPTER 11

THE ETERNAL PLAYGROUND

From Germany they came, lured by the promise of land free for the taking. First by the few, then by the score as the American Civil War came to a close. They cleared, they built, and they prospered." Researcher Brad Sundell hit this on the head, and I couldn't have said it better myself. Chippewa County in the 1800s was a time of settlement, hard work and, at times, hardships. The Henneman family was the first to actually establish a settlement in the late 1840s in Chippewa County. They set up the family farm, including a house and livestock shelter, and worked very hard to make their new life a prosperous one. Along with the farm and home, they also created a family burial plot two miles to the west of their settlement. It was close enough to care for the grounds but far enough away where they did not have to walk out of their home and feel the newfound loss wash over them.

The Emmanuel Evangelical Cemetery is located in the Tilden Township, about 4.8 miles north of Chippewa Falls on County Highway Q. According to the book *Chippewa County, Wisconsin Cemeteries*:

> *This cemetery has also been known as the Old Tilden Cemetery, the Henneman Cemetery, and the Zion Methodist Cemetery. By the year*

The Tilden Evangelical Cemetery at the turn of the last century. This is actually a copper-etched printing block from the Zion United Methodist Church, which held the original deeds to the property with the cemetery until recently. *Image courtesy of Brad Sundell.*

1863, the Emmanuel Evangelical Church was established on the cemetery site which was made up of a small wood frame in the center of the reserve. In 1894 the church was dismantled and the lumber was used to build a new church further north in Tilden. When the church was moved, the congregation split, with some staying in Tilden, and others going to a church in Chippewa Falls.

The first official recorded burial would have been Joseph Werner in 1864. The very first burials were marked by a wood rail or what Brad Sundell called "a headboard." Later burials were given marble markers, which were purchased in the nearby town of Chippewa Falls. The eastern part of the grounds was reserved for burial plots, and the first non-Hennemans were laid to rest in 1864. According to Brad Sundell's website:

Each tombstone has its own story. The Werners; a strong family of faith, were the first persons of the church. The eldest Werner is laid to rest at the southeast, with the rest of the family neatly lined up next to him. Barbara Henneman; wife of Frederick Henneman the younger, died in childbirth in 1872, at the beginning of the first diphtheria epidemic in Chippewa County. Her stillborn child was buried with her. The Bender family; John, a hero of the Civil War, died of related injuries in 1872. His son Gottlieb followed him only two years later. Rev. John Dietrich lost his wife Henrietta to diphtheria as well. Broken by the loss, he inscribed the details of her burial day upon the back of the large headstone she was laid beneath.

In 1881, there was a second outbreak of diphtheria, and it really hit the Tilden area hard, taking the lives of the majority of the children and young adults who lived in the area. Most of the interments in this cemetery are from this time, and almost all of them are children. Many families lovingly laid their little ones to rest, and some of them eventually moved away. Perhaps the loss was too much for them to bear, and they decided to plant roots away from the pain. Despite the innocence that was lost, families continued to thrive and prosper. The Hennemans sold their large farm and moved north, hoping for better land and opportunities. The final burial in the Evangelical Cemetery was the Hibbard twins in 1897. As I mentioned earlier, the church had been moved seven miles up the road to follow the congregation. The cemetery was left behind and over the years became overgrown with weeds and brambles.

While conducting research on the Internet, I stumbled across a book called *Chippewa County, Wisconsin: Past and Present*, which was available to read for free online. One individual who was laid to rest at the Evangelical Cemetery was a man by the name of Carl Duenow. According to the book:

Carl Duenow, an enterprising and progressive agriculturist, whose life of activity has been crowned with success, owns and occupies a farm of one hundred and twenty acres on section 21, Tilden township. He has lived in this county for more than a half century and he has now reached the age of seventy-nine years. However, he still gives supervision to his farm work and it is well known that his industry and intelligence have constituted the foundation upon which he has built his prosperity. He was born in Pomerania, Prussia, October 26, 1834, and is a son of Gottlieb and Dorothea Duenow, both of whom now sleep in the Evangelical Cemetery of Tilden.

The book goes on to talk about his life in great detail. In fact, the more I perused through the book, the more individuals I found who were all buried in the same cemetery. It's always interesting to read about some of the people who were buried in such a forgotten place. It really gives a feeling of humanity and also of protectiveness, which I am sure Mr. Sundell still feels to this day.

According to the book *Chippewa County, Wisconsin Cemeteries*, "Prior to 1993, it was difficult to find the graves because the cemetery had been abandoned. Bodies lay buried beneath a thick growth of brush, and it was impossible to walk through the rubble." Now fast-forward about ninety years, and we come to the year 1993. In an e-mail from Brad, he said, "My history with the cemetery started with an abandoned grave marker found behind a garage on Grand Street in Chippewa Falls. Originally, we found perhaps 4 graves there, hidden among spring lilacs. From there, we did a full survey, eventually finding about 50 graves, marked and unmarked, mostly children." A hunter, John Quilan, told Brad Sundell about the existence of the old overgrown cemetery in the woods. It might be macabre to say, but Brad was smitten with the old, battered cemetery grounds from the first moment he saw them. He decided to restore the old cemetery to its former glory. His friend Brad Demotts became interested in the restoration project as well, so they ventured over to the Chippewa County Historical Society, which provided both Brads with some partial burial listings and also put them in contact with Gladys Williams, who was the elderly daughter of the original groundskeeper. Mrs. Williams was the one who told Mr. Sundell the story behind every single burial as they came across them while cleaning up the cemetery.

According to Brad Sundell's website, he mentions how he sparked the attention of local media and film crews that came out to see what he was up to. Gladys Williams, Irma Stoffel and Brad Sundell also mapped out the entire graveyard and were able to index and record most of the plots and sections; some of them remained unknown, but so many of them had names and the graves were again claimed.

From the humble beginnings in 1993 when a lone hunter told Sundell about the old hidden cemetery all the way up until 1997, which is when the two Brads finished refurbishing the entire cemetery, this was definitely a labor of love. All the old headstones were removed and new ones created, the weeds and bramble were completely cleared and a sign was put up so after all these years, this sacred land would again be recognized. I have been in contact with Brad Sundell, who really cared so much for the cemetery that he and his friend

The Evangelical Cemetery in Tilden, circa early 1990s. *Photo courtesy of Brad Sundell.*

Brad both put so much hard work into cleaning up. Unfortunately, once it was cleared up and became known to many others, there was vandalism committed over the years. My husband, Tony, and I went to visit a couple years ago, and it was again overgrown with weeds, and headstones were smashed and pushed over. In fact, at this time we had no idea anyone had come in and done so much work to it. It makes me sad to think of all the hard work and respect to the dead, and what followed was disrespect, not only to the persons buried there, but also the two men who were so hard-working that they even camped in the cemetery on several occasions. At this point, I would like to say that vandalism is so incredibly disrespectful to the loved ones buried there, for the families who have loved ones interred and also to the good Samaritans who clean these locations up, expecting nothing in return.

As mentioned, the majority of people buried there are infants of young adults. I like to imagine that on some nights, perhaps the children come out to play and frolic about the cemetery, having fun and playing all the games they would have played in life. I spoke with friend and psychic Tamara who visited the cemetery several years ago. She stated in an e-mail, "It just felt like they were there aware of the fact we couldn't see them in the flesh. They were sadder about the kids not being able to play with them and the energy lightened up when they knew they could feel them and when our kids started talking to them." Tamara's daughter Emily was one of the children who communicated with the spirit children. A personal friend of mine, Chris Wiener is co-founder of the paranormal investigative team the Chippewa Valley Paranormal Investigators and has also written a few books of his own. He and his team, along with Tamara, did an investigation at the old Evangelical Cemetery and had some interesting stories to tell. In Wiener's book *Spirits of the Chippewa*, he states, "Tamara was picking up a lot of sadness, which would seem natural, given the nature of where we were. But then the EMF meter began to light up, telling us the storm was getting closer, or there were spirits with us. We wrapped up our mini investigation and went home." Due to the storm clouds rolling in, they had to hightail it out

Sign for the Tilden Evangelical Cemetery, 2012. *Photo courtesy of the Bells' personal collection.*

of there, but when they got home and started going over evidence, Chris claimed:

> *We began to review the video and audio. At one point Brittni stated that she was getting EMF spikes of 1.5 milligauss. Right after that, I heard one of the saddest EVPs I have ever heard in all my years of being a paranormal investigator. The EVP said this: "If we were alive they'd play with us." There were several other EVPs but none as loud and clear as this one.*

Depending on whom one speaks to, some may state there *are* spirits at the Emmanuel Evangelical Cemetery. However, it may be just be a peaceful shrine to the loved ones who were taken from their families, some of them young who never had the chance to really start living their lives. Perhaps due to the vandalism, some spirits are uneasy and feel the need to watch over the graveyard for fear of future vandals. Brad Sundell told me in an e-mail:

> *If there would be hypothetical hauntings and unrest there, it may be because of the missing stones. A wrought iron "gate" marker was stolen from there in 1996. One of the two iron crosses there went missing by 2007. The wooden markers likely rotted away seventy years ago. And we never found the markers for 4 people recorded buried there. I found a fragment or two, but no complete tablet.*

Unfinished business, vandalism or maybe not even knowing that they have passed on are reasons enough to believe this old graveyard could be haunted. But I'd like to think that if it is haunted, it is a sort of eternal playground for all those children who passed away from diphtheria many years ago. We could look at this as sad that they lost their lives at a tender age or perhaps can just think of them all playing together, just as they would have in life.

CHAPTER 12

ASK THE LIBRARIAN

Under the direction of Allen Abrams, superintendent of the Presbyterian Sunday
School, Cornell has achieved a library of which any small town might feel
justifiably proud.
—Eau Claire Leader Telegram, *October 1925*

The Cornell Library is located in the small rural town of Cornell, Wisconsin. Over the past few years, I have come across some websites that list this library as haunted, but the rest is very vague. So I decided to e-mail the librarian to see if she had anything to report. The library director, Sharon, was very helpful and sent me a historical packet she had just put together because of the town's centennial celebration in 2013. When asked about the meager accounts of ghost lore she stated:

> *I know there have been rumors of the building being haunted. I*
> *have worked here for almost fifteen years and have never experienced*
> *anything. I think the haunting rumors deal with the basement area,*
> *which was the police department, jail and fire department. It is*
> *currently just storage. I do keep things down there and am frequently*

in the basement but have never noticed anything. None of our other current employees have ever experienced anything either.

After her e-mail, I was left with the same question: is the Cornell City Library *really* haunted?

The library was started by the Presbyterian Sunday school in August 1924. The superintendent, Allen Abrams, had a vision of opening a library that would be available to all citizens. Abrams did a canvass for a small number of books that would become the nucleus for a Sunday school library. Throughout the first year the library was open, it expanded with the help of book campaigns and drives, which were sponsored by the Sunday school. Students from the school were placed on teams with the goal of trying to obtain books or money to help start the library. These students worked odd jobs around town, and some communicated in letters to friends and family who did not live around the area, asking for donations of "good books." As the library expanded, it was accessible one day a week for townspeople to come in and open their minds to the world of reading.

In 1925, Mr. Abrams realized the library had grown so much that it would no longer fit within the Presbyterian church. He also felt that a new building should be in a more centralized location because it would encourage everyone to use the library. According to the historical packet the library director gave me:

Allen Abrams approached the Cornell Women's Club to ask if they would take over the library. With support from the Village Board, the American Legion, the Cornell Wood Products Company, and the Board of Education, the Women's club agreed to take on the library. The plan was to locate the library on the main floor of the Einar Woll building (which is now the old Ben Franklin store) on Main Street. With the move, the library was open two afternoons and two evenings each week.

The Cornell Public Library, year unknown. *Photo courtesy of the Cornell Public Library.*

This, along with many other fundraisers and events, gave the library a new home, a better location and many more reading materials that residents could enjoy for years to come.

Cornell built a new Village Hall in the year 1928, which is the home of the Cornell Library today. The library moved into this new building on December 6, 1928. The first floor, or basement of the new Village Hall, was used for a furnace room, fire hall, jail and restroom. The second floor was used for the actual library and village council room. This entire area was separated by a large folding door so when the council was not in use, the door could be moved to the side and open up the whole floor for the library. During May and into the summer of 1928, the library was closed because of the scarlet fever epidemic. All books were brought back to the library, and the books that were in homes of families with the fever were burned. The remaining books that were brought back to the library were disinfected before the building opened once again.

Many thanks to library director Sharon for providing me with so much historical information on this building. After reading through her pamphlet, I was still left with many questions regarding any paranormal activity at the library. I took to perusing the Internet again and finally found a story on a website that was written by an individual named Michael. This is what he had to say:

> *The small city library in Cornell is a location that triggers unease in most any one that enters it. As far as the history of the building goes, the basement where the restroom is, used to be a jail during the earlier duration of Cornell's existence. The entire building has a heavy sort of a feeling to it but it is the basement in particular that makes all who step down there to visit the restroom uneasy. Some librarians working there would not go down to the basement to the bathroom the entire time they worked there because of the uncomfortable feeling that overwhelms visitors to the basement. The entire basement area has had virtually no remodeling and is for lack of a better description, "rugged." To my knowledge there have been no sightings of any kind, just the feeling of an overbearing presence of some kind.*

The Cornell Library is rich in both history and literature. Some individuals out there would say that this building houses not just books but spirits as well, which may have caused unease for past patrons, especially within the old basement walls. I still am left with my unanswered question as to whether this place really is haunted. However, when it comes to the paranormal, I think we all would like to believe the answer is out there. But if we were able to solve each and every mystery about places we have heard, read about or visited, wouldn't that ruin the allure of how or why these locations are reported to be haunted? In the case of the Cornell City Library, there isn't much information out there that speaks of any personal accounts, which makes me wonder if the stories of the supernatural here are simply just that: stories.

BIBLIOGRAPHY

"About Augusta Wisconsin." http://www.augustawi.com/about/about. html.

"About the House." House of Rock. http://www.house-of-rock.com/.

"Asylum Cemetery." http://www.findagrave.com/cgi-bin/fg.cgi?page=cr& CRid=2212481.

Barland, L. *Sawdust City: A History of Eau Claire, Wisconsin from the earliest times to 1910.* Stevens Point, WI: Worzalla Publishing Company, 1960.

Bauer, B. "Woman Found Stabbed to Death." *Leader Telegram*, February 16, 1974.

Berg, B. "Best Local Urban Legend." Volume One. http://volumeone. org/news/15/posts/2009/09/18/1204_BEST_LOCAL_URBAN_ LEGEND.

Bloms, J. "*The James Sheeley House Restaurant and Saloon.*" http://www. jamessheeleyhouse.com/.

"Bloomer Massacre?" Unexplained Research. http://chadlewis. proboards.com/index.cgi?board=legendtrippers&action=display&thr ead=1764.

Chronicle Telegram. "Town Talks of Deer and Mass Murder," November 22, 1981.

"Cornell, Wisconsin Ghost Sightings." Ghosts of America. http://www. ghostsofamerica.com/5/Wisconsin_Cornell_ghost_sightings.html.

Curtiss-Wedge, F., and G.O. Jones. *The History of Dunn County, Wisconsin, Volume 2.* N.p.: H.C. Cooper, Jr. & Company, 1925.

Daily Independent. "Killed By Fall in Eau Claire," May 24, 1910.

Dewitz, T. "Site of the Old Tilden Emmanuel Evangelical Church and Cemetery." Travis Dewitz Photography. http://www.dewitzphotography.com/eau-claire-wi-photographer/site-of-the-old-tilden-emmanuel-evangelical-church-and-cemetery-founded-1868/.

"Eau Claire County Asylum and Home for the Poor." Eau Claire Co. WIGenWeb. http://eauclaire.wigenweb.org/histories/1914ecco/chapter19/asylum.htm.

Eau Claire Weekly Leader. November 2, 1895.

"Eau Claire, Wisconsin Ghost Sightings." Ghosts of America. http://www.ghostsofamerica.com/5/Wisconsin_Eau_Claire_ghost_sightings.html.

"Emmanuel Evangelical Cemetery." http://www.findagrave.com/cgi-bin/fg.cgi?page=cr&CRid=1981381.

"Emmanuel Evangelical Cemetery Tilden." In D.M. Bourget and A.M. Society, *Chippewa County Wisconsin Cemeteries.* Chippewa Falls, WI, 1998.

"Evelyn Hartley." La Crosse Public Library Digital Library Collection. http://www.lacrosselibrary.org/digital_archives/digitalproject/hartley.htm.

Fefer, A. "Paranormal Investigation: Do You Believe in Ghosts?" WEAU. COM. http://www.weau.com/home/headlines/67760207.html.

Gharrity, B. "Two Dead, One Wounded After Shootings in City." *Leader Telegram,* April 16, 1981.

Gonyea family. "*Chippewa Falls Train Crash 1924.*" http://www.gonyeafamily.com/gonyea/item/97-chippewa-falls-train-crash-1924.html.

Guyette, M. "Elk Mound, Wisconsin: Dead Mailmen Haunted Castle." http://www.roadsideamerica.com/tip/30733.

Haake, K. "*County Q Cemetery, Tilden, Chippewa County, WI.*" USGENWEB Archives. http://files.usgwarchives.net/wi/chippewa/cemeteries/countyq.txt.

History of Chippewa County, Wisconsin: Past and Present, Vol. II. Chicago: S.J. Clarke Publishing Company, 1913.

Juliano, D., and T. Carlson. "Haunted Places in Wisconsin." The Shadowlands. http://www.theshadowlands.net/places/wisconsin.htm.

Lewis, C. "Drowned in Chippewa May 16, 1905." Volume One. http://volumeone.org/news/1/posts/2010/05/14/1608_Drowned_in_Chippewa_May_16_1905.

Lewis, Chad, and Terry Fisk. *The Wisconsin Road Guide to Haunted Locations.* Eau Claire: Unexplained Publishing LLC, 2004.

Manning, J. "Chippewa River Soo Line Trestle." Bridge Hunter. http://bridgehunter.com/wi/chippewa/bh43025.

Milwaukee Journal. "Trial Ordered in Stabbing Death," January 24, 1986.

"Minneapolis, St. Paul & Sault Ste. Marie Railway." In *Summary of Accident Investigation Reports.* Washington: Washington Government Printing Office, 1925.

Novitzke, C. "Checking In on Favorite Haunts in Chippewa Falls." Wisconsinosity.com. http://www.wisconsinosity.com/Chippewa/articles/checking_in_on_favorite_haunts_i.htm.

"Paranormal Actvity at the Sheeley House Tavern." Most Haunted Places in America. http://www.ghosteyes.com/paranormal-activity-sheeley-house-tavern.

Petersen, B. Evelyn Hartley. Interview with the author, 2012.

Racer, Theresa. "Theresa's Haunted History of the Tri-State." http://theresashauntedhistoryofthetri-state.blogspot.com/2012/09/elk-lake-dam-wisconsin.html.

Shepard, S. Cornell Public Library. Interview with the author, November 26, 2012.

———. "The Cornell Public Library: A Short History." Cornell, WI: self-published pamphlet, 2013.

Smoot, F. "Thanks for Asking." Volume One. http://volumeone.org/articles/2010/11/18/1861_Thanks_for_Asking_Nov_18_2010.

Springer-Gleason, T. Emmanuel Evangelical Cemetery. Interview with the author, December 2012.

Staff, S. *Have to See It to Believe It.* Unexplained Research. http://www.unexplainedresearch.com/media/have_to_see_it_to_believe_it.html.

Stetzer, R. "Fox Family Turns Items for Life on the Road into Business." *Chippewa Herald*. http://chippewa.com/news/local/fox-family-turns-items-for-life-on-the-road-into/article_3c4ca012-92af-11e0-b5a6-001cc4c03286.html.

Sundell, B. Emmanuel Evangelical Cemetery. Interviewer with the author, 2012.

———. "Emmanuel Evangelical Cemetery." The Whole Magilla. http://thewholemagilla.tripod.com/id68.html.

"*The Haunted Man* Quotes." LitQuotes. http://www.litquotes.com/quote_title_resp.php?TName=The%20Haunted%20Man.

Wiener, C. *Eisold's Irvine Bar*. Chippewa Valley Paranormal Investigators. http://www.chippewavpi.com/Log_Irvine_Bar.html.

Wiener, C., and C. Rice. *Haunted Chippewa Falls*. Chippewa Falls, WI: CVPI, 2009.

Wiener, C., C. Rice and team. *Spirits of the Chippewa*. Chippewa Falls, WI: CVPI, 2012.

Wolfert, W. "*Opera House Once Cultural Center*." US Gen Net. http://www.usgennet.org/usa/wi/county/eauclaire/history/ourstory/vol4/opera.html.

ABOUT THE AUTHOR

D evon Bell currently resides in the midst of the Chippewa Valley and calls Eau Claire, Wisconsin, her home. There she lives with her husband, Tony, and two cats, Minnie and Mattie. Devon, alongside her husband, is co-owner of the Haunting Experiments, which has put out many historical/paranormal documentaries, including a hit web series called "The Haunting Experiments Web Series." She is a paranormal researcher and writer and has narrated, acted and directed several paranormal film projects. She also released a full-length historical/paranormal documentary called *Caryville: A Documentary*, which she produced alongside her husband. This has led to her sharing some of the mysteries and horrors of creepy Caryville in this very book.

Along with the paranormal, Devon also has written and directed a full-length feature film, along with other short films as well. She is an accomplished singer and has been involved with musical theater, performed at many weddings and also spent some time in recording studios. She is a lover of Andrew Lloyd Webber's hit musical *The Phantom of the Opera* and is an avid collector of memorabilia and period/historical costumes. Mrs. Bell has always been fascinated with history and ghost lore and feels that through preserving both, there will be so much more to offer future generations to come.